Disclaimer

This book is intended for information purposes only. The author does not promise or imply any results to those using this information, nor are they responsible for any adverse results brought about by the usage of the information contained herein. Use the information provided at your own risk. Furthermore, the author does not guarantee that the holder of this information will improve his or her health from the information contained herein.

The author of this book has used his/her best efforts in preparing this book. The author makes no representation of warranties with respect to the accuracy, applicability, or completeness of the contents of this book.

© 2025 CAD Graphics, In

ISBN: 978-1-958837-36-8

Intelligence   Wellness

(Knowledge & Adaptation)   (Health & Fitness)

Mind   Body

Spirit

Meaning-Purpose-Community

Self-awareness

We are the architect of our own health, happiness, destiny, or fate.

Foreword

I am excited to present *The Wellness Chronicles*, a culmination of insights gathered from my many past years of writing on holistic health. This book distills key concepts from hundreds of my articles, offering a practical and thought-provoking guide to achieving well-being through a balanced approach to life.

In today's fast-paced world, where stress and pharmaceutical dependency often overshadow self-care and preventative health, *The Wellness Chronicles* serves as a beacon for those seeking a deeper understanding of the mind-body-spirit connection. It explores a broad spectrum of topics, including nutrition, physiology, healthcare modalities, meditation, psychology, and philosophy, all with an underlying focus on empowering individuals to take charge of their own well-being.

Readers will discover time-honored healing traditions such as Traditional Chinese Medicine (TCM) and Ayurveda, alongside modern holistic approaches that emphasize balance and harmony. This book encourages self-awareness and practical application, addressing injuries and ailments through natural, non-pharmaceutical solutions while advocating for movement, breathwork, and mindfulness as essential tools for health.

Beyond physical well-being, *The Wellness Chronicles* delves into the intricate connections between mind and body—how emotions, thought patterns, and beliefs influence our nervous system, stress responses, and overall vitality. These principles are supported by both ancient wisdom and contemporary insights, illustrating the profound interplay between psychology, philosophy, and personal transformation.

As a visual complement to these insights, I have included many of my original graphics throughout the book. These illustrations highlight self-regulation techniques, eclectic exercises, and Eastern methodologies, demonstrating how the intentional control of breath (wind), circulation (water), and mental focus can cultivate resilience, restore balance, and increase vitality (fire), a reflection of the Taoist concept that *"wind and water create fire."*

The Wellness Chronicles is more than a guide. It is an invitation to reflect, explore, and apply holistic principles in everyday life. My hope is that this book serves as both a resource and an inspiration, encouraging deeper inquiry into the art of living well.

Thank you for your engagement with this work. I am eager to share this journey with you and contribute to the collective pursuit of enduring health, happiness, and fulfillment.

Sincerely,

Jim Moltzan

Why I Share, What I Have Learned

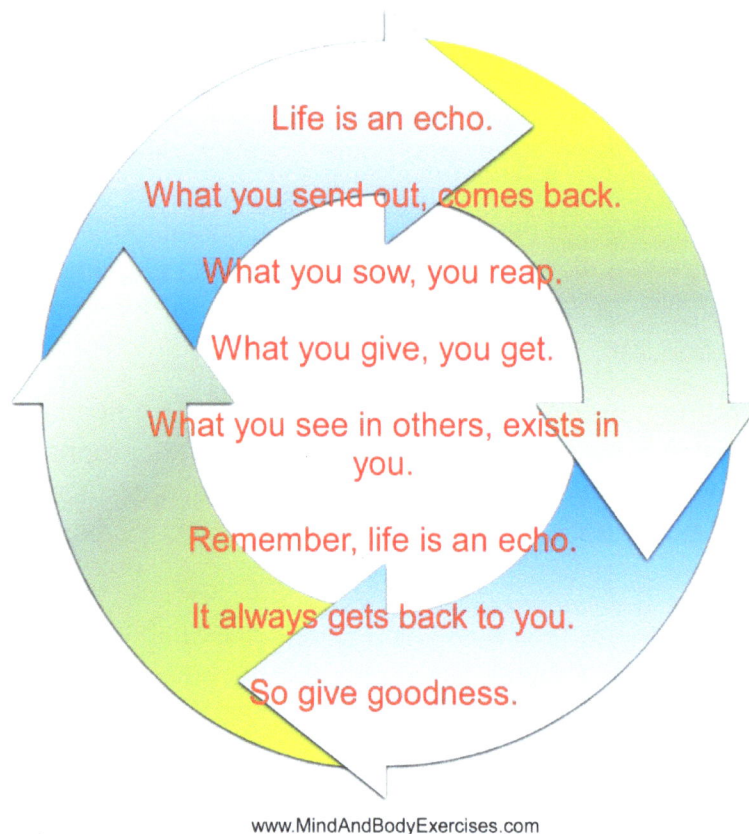

Life is an echo.

What you send out, comes back.

What you sow, you reap.

What you give, you get.

What you see in others, exists in you.

Remember, life is an echo.

It always gets back to you.

So give goodness.

www.MindAndBodyExercises.com

I made my commitment many years ago to learn, study, practice and teach fitness and well-being. My education came from martial arts and various other Eastern methods rooted in Traditional Chinese Medicine (TCM). I started when I was 16 years old and have never stopped since; 61 now.

I have written journals, produced educational graphics and co-authored a book in addition to many that I have self-authored. I blog often with a WordPress site, writing about the anatomical, physiological and mental benefits of mind and body training. Years back I started recording my classes and lectures, knowing that somewhere down the line, all of this information would be valuable to those who need and desire it.

My YouTube channel has almost 300 videos of FREE classes and other education videos. The goal all along has been to raise the awareness that Tai chi (a martial art), qigong (yoga at its root) and many other Eastern wellness methods, have proven the test of time for maintaining well-being. No gym, no mat, no membership, no special clothes or equipment. Just the individual and their engagement. Weak or injured knees, back issues (strains & sciatica), stress & anxiety, asthma, arthritis, balance, poor posture - the list is endless. These are all issues that can be improved or overcome by those serious about learning about the mind, body & spirit connection.

Table of Contents

Human Behavior

Conspiracy Mentality – Huh, what is this?

Conspiracy mentality is a generalized belief that secret and powerful forces aspire to control or rule the world. A lack of control has been identified as one of the driving forces of conspiracy beliefs. When people fear a lack of control in their lives, they compensate for this deficiency by seeking patterns, even if these patterns are based on illusion. Events of a large magnitude warrant an explanation of comparable proportions. Studies conducted in both the USA and the UK showed the belief that Covid19 is a hoax or a stronger belief that the virus originated in a medical laboratory (Imhoff & Lamberty 2020).

A Neuroscientist Explains What Conspiracy Theories Do To Your Brain Video | Technology Networks

Conspiracy theories are not supported by sound evidence but rather are based on various thinking patterns that are known to be unreliable tools for tracking reality. True conspiracies are revealed through available evidence of actual and verifiable events, along with a healthy dose of skepticism. People might look to a particular conspiracy of scientists to explain a general scientific conclusion when it aligns with their political ideology, but not when the scientific consensus has no relevance to their own politics (Lewandowsky & Cook 2020).

Not all conspiracies are false theories, as many were actually true such as the US government poisoning alcohol during Prohibition, to discourage people from drinking booze, the CIA testing behavior modification using LSD and other hallucinogenic drugs on Americans in a top-secret experiment, and the Gulf of Tonkin incident of 1964, which was faked to encourage American support for the Vietnam War (Cahn 2021). Another proven conspiracy is The Tuskegee Syphilis Experiment, which speaks volumes of how America's medical culture has used race as a way to wield power for its own personal gain (Lombardo, 2006). The list continues with "Operation Berkshire": the international tobacco companies' conspiracy, where the industry's commercial interests were protected by both promoting controversy over smoking and disease and through strategies directed at reassuring smokers (Francey & Chapman 2000).

Or when the AMA got caught conspiring to "contain and eliminate the chiropractic profession. As reported in Marc Micozzi's *Fundamentals of Complementary, Alternative, and Integrative Medicine: A staunchly anti-chiropractic policy was pursued by the American Medical Association (AMA). In 1990 the U.S. Supreme Court affirmed a lower court ruling in which the AMA was found liable for federal antitrust violations for having engaged in a conspiracy to "contain and eliminate" (the AMA's own words) the chiropractic profession (Wilk v. AMA, 1990). The process that culminated in this landmark decision began in 1974 when a large packet of confidential AMA documents was provided anonymously to leaders of the American Chiropractic Association and the International Chiropractors Association. As a result of the ensuing Wilk v. AMA litigation, the AMA reversed its long-standing ban on interprofessional cooperation between medical doctors and chiropractors, agreed to publish the full findings of the court in the Journal of the American Medical Association, and paid an undisclosed sum, most of which was earmarked for chiropractic research. This ruling has not completely reversed the effects of organized medicine's boycott, especially when it comes to the application of the most effective and cost-effective treatments for common pain conditions".*

Conspiracy mentality is interconnected to a feeling of lack of control to a perceived threat. When people feel more in control of their environment and decisions within it, they are more able to tolerate the seemingly constant ebb and flow of conspiracy theories. If people are educated to be aware of unsound reasoning found in most conspiracy theories, they have a better chance of not being influenced by such theories. When people are educated or prebunked, prior to their knowledge of a particular conspiracy, they can develop a resilience or awareness of the conspiratorial messages. Prebunking, also known as inoculation, consists of an explicit warning of an impending threat of being misled, and an objection to the misinformation's arguments (Lewandowsky & Cook 2020).

Logic-based facts can help to explain misleading methods in unsound reasoning used in conspiracy theories. Educating skeptics about the logical misconceptions found in anti-vaccination conspiracies has been found to be effective by drawing attention to vaccination research that has been conducted by independent, publicly funded scientists who can discredit conspiracy theories about the pharmaceutical industry. Fact-based information can support the fact that the conspiracy theory is false by communicating accurate data. Fact-based and logic-based inoculations have both been successful in prebunking other conspiracies such as some of those surrounding the terrorist attacks of 9/11 (Lewandowsky & Cook 2020).

CONSPIR: The seven traits of conspiratorial thinking

There are seven traits of conspiratorial thinking [29], summarized (and more easily remembered) with the acronym **CONSPIR**:

C	O	N	S	P	I	R
Contradictory	Overriding suspicion	Nefarious Intent	Something Must Be Wrong	Persecuted Victim	Immune to Evidence	Re-interpreting Randomness

Contradictory

Conspiracy theorists can simultaneously believe in ideas that are mutually contradictory. For example, believing the theory that Princess Diana was murdered but also believing that she faked her own death.[30] This is because the theorists' commitment to disbelieving the "official" account is so absolute, it doesn't matter if their belief system is incoherent.

Overriding suspicion

Conspiratorial thinking involves a nihilistic degree of skepticism towards the official account.[31] This extreme degree of suspicion prevents belief in anything that doesn't fit into the conspiracy theory.

Nefarious intent

The motivations behind any presumed conspiracy are invariably assumed to be nefarious.[31] Conspiracy theories never propose that the presumed conspirators have benign motivations.

References:

Imhoff, R. & Lamberty, P. (2020). A bioweapon or a hoax? The link between distinct conspiracy beliefs about the coronavirus disease (COVID-19) outbreak and pandemic behavior. *Social Psychological and Personality Science*.

Lewandowsky, S., & Cook, J. (2020). The Conspiracy Theory Handbook. http://sks.to/conspiracy (Links to an external site.)

Cahn, L. (2021, July 26). *12 Conspiracy Theories That Actually Turned Out to Be True*. Reader's Digest. https://www.rd.com/list/conspiracy-theories-that-turned-out-to-be-true/

Micozzi, Marc S.. Fundamentals of Complementary, Alternative, and Integrative Medicine – E-Book (p. 537). Elsevier Health Sciences. Kindle Edition

Lombardo, P. A., & Dorr, G. M. (2006). Eugenics, Medical Education, and the Public Health Service: Another Perspective on the Tuskegee Syphilis Experiment. Bulletin of the History of Medicine, 291-316.

Francey, N., & Chapman, S. (2000). "Operation Berkshire": the international tobacco companies' conspiracy. *BMJ (Clinical research ed.)*, *321*(7257), 371–374. https://doi.org/10.1136/bmj.321.7257.371

Situational Awareness
Basic Self-defense Skills

Use Knowledge, Not Fear

We live in a very different world than when we were young adults, years ago. We see television and movies where everyone seems to know kung fu or have awesome skills, but in reality, most kids (and adults) never learn how to defend themselves these days until after the actual need arises – which unfortunately could be too late. Hiding under a table and waiting for help isn't always the best option when an attacker already has their hands around someone's throat.

Good skills to learn:

- Basic defense skills against be grabbed, touched, punched, etc.

- Anatomy relative to "pressure points" or key body parts to defend or attack if necessary.

- Situational awareness relative to options before and after someone finds themselves in a potentially dangerous and life changing event.

- Balance, coordination and strength exercises to develop self-esteem and confidence that one does not need to be a victim or rely upon others for their own personal safety.

5

If You Have Never Had to Defend Yourself, Nor Practiced Self-defense - How Do You Know What You Will Do?

Typical Ways People Are Assaulted

Choke (front)

Choke (behind)

Double Shoulder (behind)

Double Shoulder (front)

Punch to Face

Same Side Wrist

Cross Side Wrist

Double Wrists (behind)

Double Wrists (front)

Sitting On Top

Bear Hug (behind)

Bear Hug (front)

Knife Lunge

Knife on Throat

Self-awareness & Self-defense are skills that can be practiced to improve success

www.MindAndBodyExercises.com

Do You Know How You Will React if Facing Danger

If you have never driven a car, how do you know if you can actually get it moving and then navigate safely?

If you have never had to fix a flat tire, how do you do it when no one is around, and you are stuck in the middle of nowhere?

So how does someone defend themselves or their loved ones, if they have never been in a dangerous situation?

Well, you can learn how to ahead of time so you can be prepared. Or wait and figure it out as you go.

Have you ever heard "failing to prepare" vs. "prepare to fail"?

For more information on this topic, look at my video at: https://youtu.be/oHFM_EjhO6A

Do Nothing or Do Something

So, you might have some chronic pain issues, persistent balance problems (physically and/or mentally) or maybe even a negative outlook of where your life trajectory is going - what do you do?

1) do nothing
2) do nothing, but complain
3) seek medical treatment, followed with medications
4) look in the mirror, dig deep and realize that you are in charge of your own well-being (accountability & self-discipline)
5) take the steps to adjust your lifestyle to improve the root problems of your issues

Every year, a new year comes and goes by, while many look for a new resolution but eventually fall back to poor habits. A goal, a path and a teacher can help cultivate the self-discipline that it takes to be happy.

The following graphics offer some insight into why many suffer from chronic pain and a few options to help.

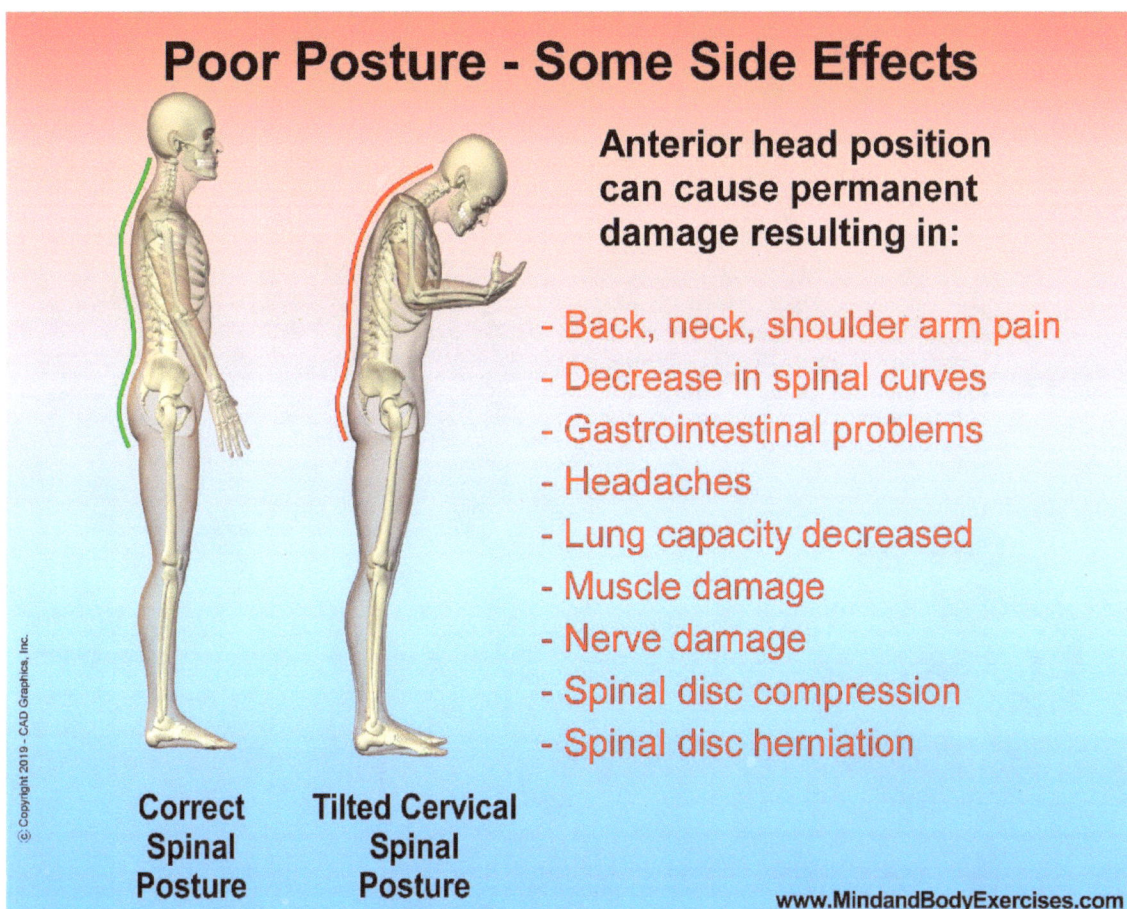

Poor Posture - Some Side Effects

Anterior head position can cause permanent damage resulting in:

- Back, neck, shoulder arm pain
- Decrease in spinal curves
- Gastrointestinal problems
- Headaches
- Lung capacity decreased
- Muscle damage
- Nerve damage
- Spinal disc compression
- Spinal disc herniation

Correct Spinal Posture

Tilted Cervical Spinal Posture

© Copyright 2019 - CAD Graphics, Inc.

www.MindandBodyExercises.com

Instinctively, as humans we try to center our head directly above our physical center of gravity. Poor posture, short leg syndrome, injuries or habitual body movements can cause remodeling of the muscular, skeletal and nervous system. These root problems can be the cause of many chronic ailments.

A difference in leg length by 7mm or 0.275" can be enough to throw an individual's spine out of "calibration".

Side effects can include:
- headaches
- neck pain
- shoulder pain
- low back pain
- hip pain
- Iliotibial Band Syndrome
- knee pain
- ankle/foot pain

Other Causes:
- wallet in rear pocket
- uneven/inferior footwear
- tight calves, hamstrings, etc.
- excessive use of right or left sides
- career related

0.275

Shoulder pain can occur when ones side of the body is higher or lower than the opposite side.

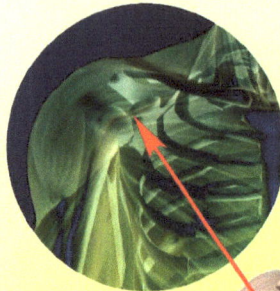

Line of Center of Gravity

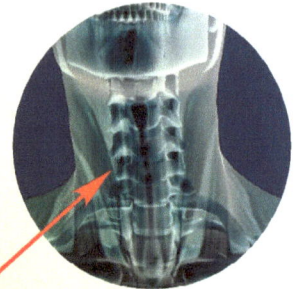

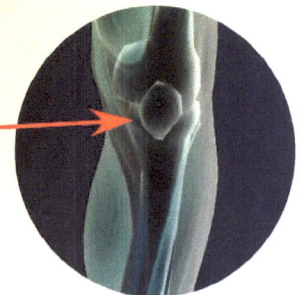

Neck pain and headaches can occur when one side of the neck has more tension than the opposite.

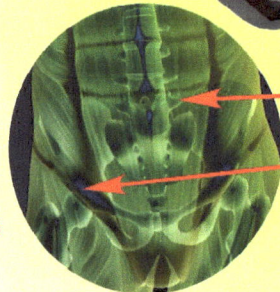

Center of Gravity

Knee, hip and iliotibial band pain can occur when ones body weight is unevenly distributed between the two legs.

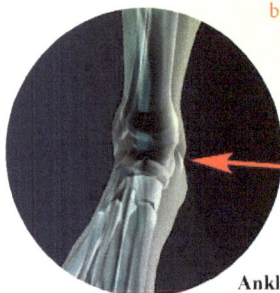

Ankle pain can occur when ones side of the body is favored due to chronic pain.

Knee pain can occur when ones body weight is unevenly distributed between the two legs.

NOTE: This study guide is a general reference for the concepts shown.

Course of Action:

- consult with your physician or chiropractor
- have your posture checked
- stretch regularly
- perform non-specific symmetrical exercises
- inspect footware for uneven wear patterns
- evaluate poor posture habits and adjust
- review career choices if necessary

Chronic pain effects us emotionally (mentally) as well as physically. Similar to a sponge, the body absorbs positive as well as negative energy. Each emotion effects an internal organ.

Liver - anger, depression
Heart - lack of joy
Spleen - worry
Lung - grief
Kidney - fear

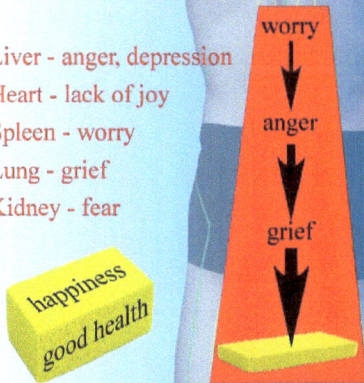

worry

anger

grief

happiness
good health

There are twelve main medians and 8 other special meridians within the human body. Meridians are similar to electrical wires or nerves. They run from the top of the head to the tips of the toes and finger. Each meridian is associated with an internal organ. When there is a lack of flow or blockage within the meridians, health problems can arise. Through proper diet, exercises and lifestyle, it is possible to keep the chi flowing through the meridians.

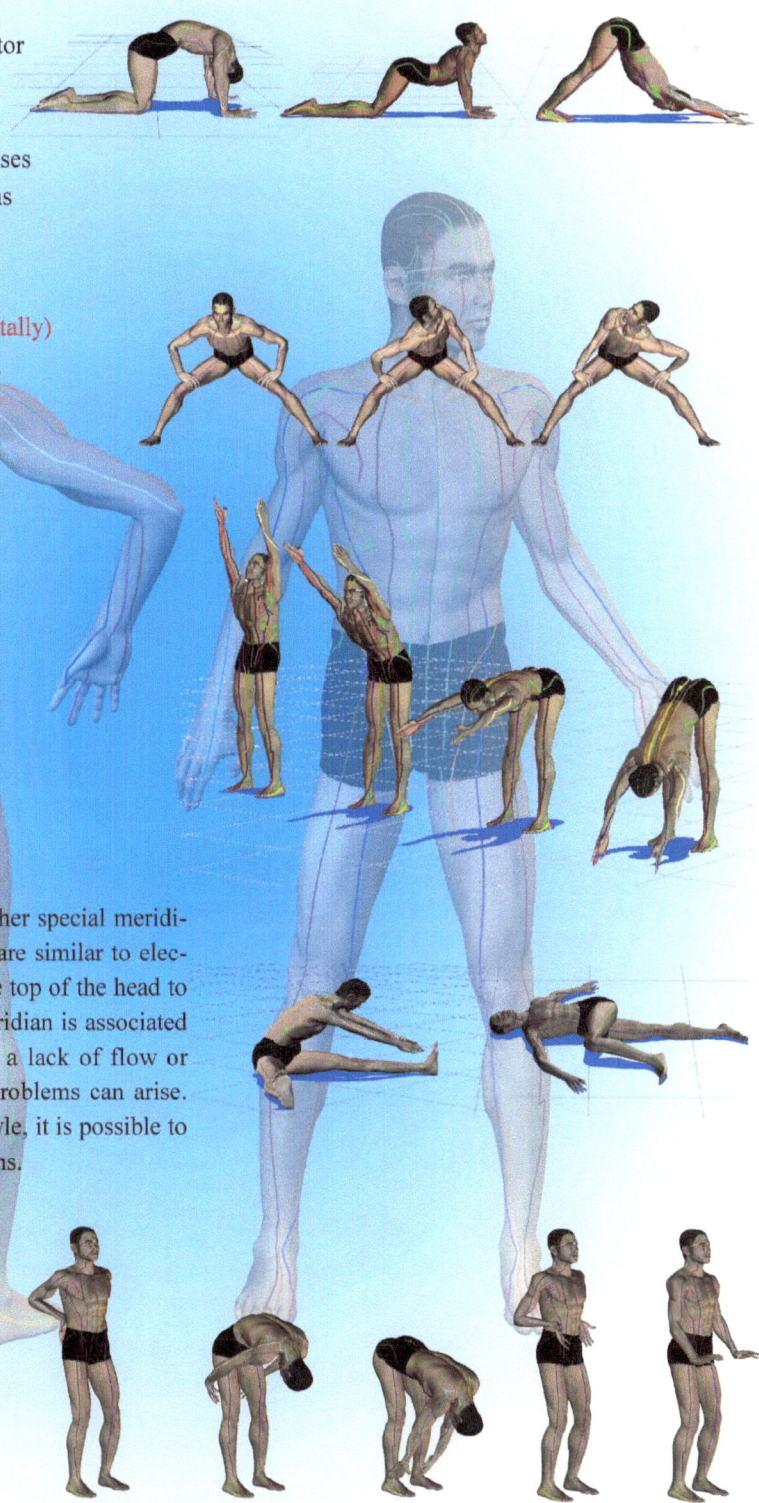

NOTE: This study guide is a general reference for the concepts shown.

9

Get Your Jab, and if You Behave You Get a Free COOKIE!

WOW, free goodies from Budweiser, Junior's Cheesecake, Krispy Kreme, Nathan's Hot Dogs, White Castle and others for getting a jab.

Seems so gracious on the surface. Good marketing ploy and press for the junk food industry. But really counterproductive in principle if we truly are trying not to be sick, these are 1st items we should remove from our diet. Being healthy is not the same as not being sick.

Excessive consumption of junk food (low nutritional value items), and abuse of alcohol, help cause diabetes, heart disease, obesity, and other comorbidities, **WHICH ARE** the leading risk factors with COVID-19. Being part of the solution shouldn't really contribute to the root problems of poor diet & lifestyle.

Instead, maybe give out free vitamins and a brochure on how to live a healthier life through better nutrition, consistent exercise, management of stress, fresh air, healthy social interactions, sunlight, connection with nature, a sense of purpose.

Got vaccinated?

Here's all the free stuff you can get that is truly terrible for your health:

Got vaccinated? Here's all the free stuff you can get that is truly terrible for your health:
https://www.cnn.com/.../business/vaccine-freebies/index.html

CNN.COM

Got vaccinated? Here's all the free stuff you can get
After surviving a fear-filled year of the Covid-19 pandemic, getting ...

Health Care & Personal Responsibility – Cost vs. Value

A very conflicted current subject is about how much Americans spend on health care for what doesn't always amount to better health. As a nation, we are spending more every year on health-related expenses ($13,000+), while our average adult weight has increased 30 pounds since 1950. Often, I enter into discussions regarding how much it is appropriate to charge for fitness options such as wellness classes, health club memberships and various other related services.

Annual U.S. Healthcare Expenses per Person by Year

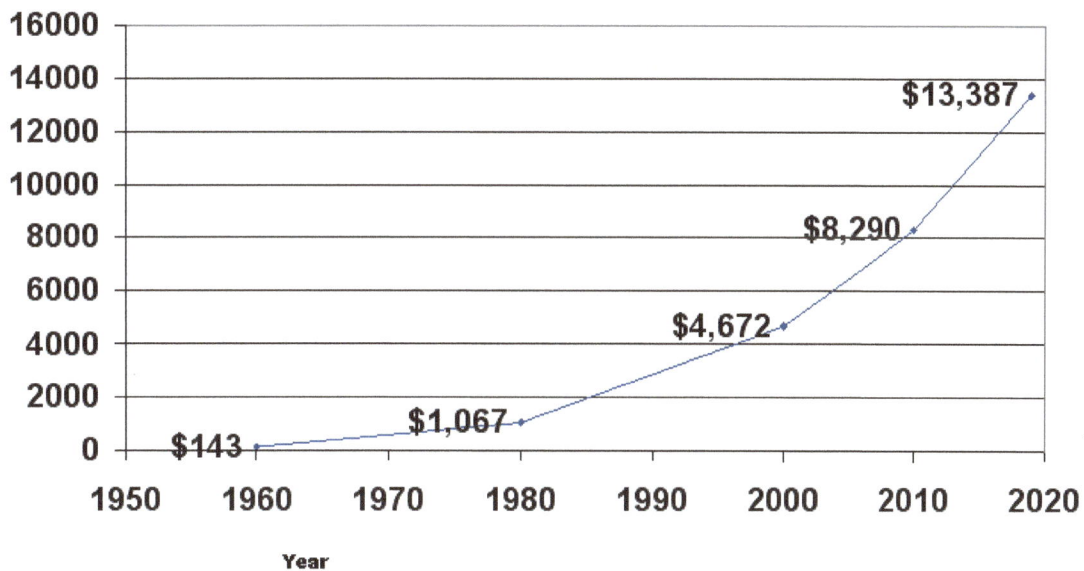

Source: http://www1.cms.gov/NationalHealthExpendData/downloads/proj2009.pdf

We usually look for the best value for the money we spend on whatever commodity we seek. When purchasing a service do you look for the best price or the best quality? Or perhaps a balance of the two? When seeking a dentist or doctor do you choose the cheapest? The cheapest vehicle? The cheapest education? Or the best value for your money?

What makes the difference between a house made of wood versus a brick house? Or the benefit of a healthy home cooked meal over fast food? An exercise video over an actual teacher? Group classes over individual instruction. Time and experience give us the wisdom that cheaper is not always better. The easy path is usually not the better choice in the long run.

When offering group fitness classes (tai chi or qigong) for free (or cost under $10), I have generally found that working adults do not associate much value with the education that I share at this price point. I understand their viewpoint that because it is free or cheap, why commit to attending? There is no consequence whether they show up or not. However, when people prepay or commit to a specific period of time, they feel more commitment to getting their money's worth. When I charge $50 or more for a 1-hour private class, the student receives greater benefits because they have ownership in participating in and getting the results that they are paying for. When a student commits to a month or years' worth of goal-oriented training, we are both now committed to seeing it through to achieve that goal. It is so cliché, but I have found more often than not, you do get what you pay for.

Mind & Body Training Return on Investment

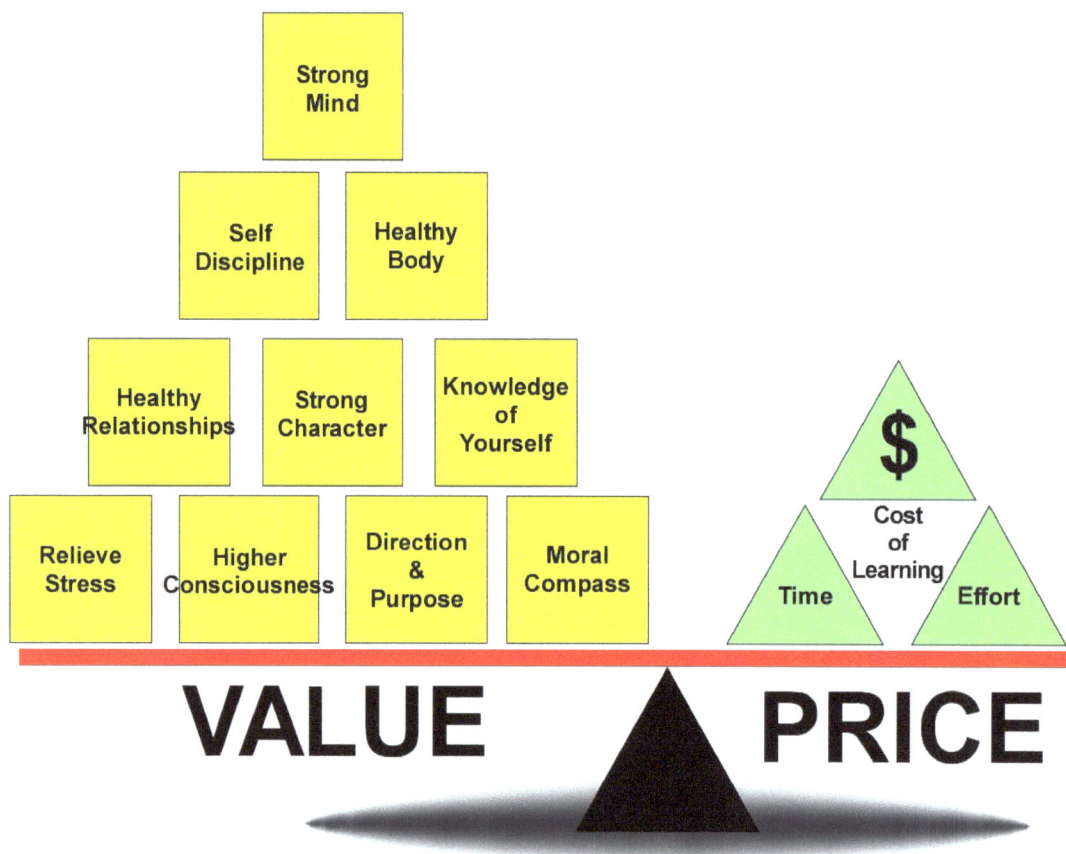

```
                    Strong
                     Mind

            Self            Healthy
          Discipline         Body

     Healthy      Strong    Knowledge
   Relationships  Character     of
                            Yourself

  Relieve    Higher     Direction   Moral         $
  Stress  Consciousness     &      Compass
                         Purpose            Cost
                                       Time  of   Effort
                                           Learning
```

VALUE ▲ PRICE

Why do I lean towards martial arts, tai chi, qigong and yoga? Personally, I have not found anything else that offers such a wide palette of benefits than the mind, body and spirit type of exercises. Every exercise method has its pros and cons, but the aforementioned encourage the individuals of **ALL AGES** to become more self-aware and make adjustments as necessary to avoid injuries or other issues. Strength, flexibility, balance, coordination – all can be challenged more or less depending upon the individuals' age, goals and abilities. Other benefits such as stress relief, mental clarity, self-defense skills, confidence and chronic pain management are difficult to put a price tag upon. Also, there is no need for expensive equipment nor a special location to train, make for an attractive option in lieu of a pricey membership at the local upscale health club.

While some will need to continue to invest monetarily to their portfolio to insure, they have enough resources to pay for future health insurance, co-pays, prescriptions and over the counter meds, others will choose to invest in their own "health care program". Pursuing an education in how to take care of oneself is indeed a wise investment.

More statistics backing up a need to be proactive in your healthcare:

An ABC News report from 2012 states that:

"A new report estimates that the average American worker spends nearly $14.40 a week on coffee, which does not include the cost of drinking coffee at home. Data is shown to indicate that the average worker spends around $1,100 annually on coffee."

This is more than most Americans spend on their own fitness goals throughout the year.

https://abcnews.go.com/GMA/american-coffee-habits-spend-coffee/story?id=16923079

USA Today reported in 2016:

"The average gym membership costs just under $60 per month, and 67% of memberships go unused. Meanwhile, memberships to specialized workouts like Crossfit have the fit-minded shelling out hundreds per month."

https://www.usatoday.com/story/money/personalfinance/2016/04/27/your-gym-membership-good-investment/82758866/

A CBS News report from 2014 states:

"A new government study estimates that nearly 80 percent of adult Americans do not get the recommended amounts of exercise each week, potentially setting themselves up for years of health problems."

https://www.cbsnews.com/news/cdc-80-percent-of-american-adults-dont-get-recommended-exercise/

Intrinsic vs. Extrinsic Motivation

Self-reflection can lead one to contemplate how motivated they are to accomplish specific tasks and goals.

How Are You Motivated?

Intrinsic

Fun

Growth

Passion

Self-expression

Enjoyment

Curiosity

Purpose

**Interest or satisfaction
in executing the task itself**

Intrinsic motivation is executing an activity for its own sake. Enjoy the activity because it is fun, satisfying or challenging. Not because you'll get a reward or avoid punishment.

Extrinsic

Bonuses
Promotions

Recognition

Raises

Benefits

Praise
Prizes
Perks

**Results are an outcome of
executing the task**

Extrinsic motivation is doing something not because you enjoy it, but rather because you want to receive a reward or avoid punishment. This is the opposite of intrinsic motivation.

www.MindandBodyExercises.com

© Copyright 2020 - CAD Graphics, Inc.

Intrinsic Motivation:

Intrinsic motivation is executing an activity for its own sake. Enjoy the activity because it is fun, satisfying or challenging. Not because you'll get a reward or avoid punishment.

Extrinsic Motivation:

Extrinsic motivation is doing something not because you enjoy it, but rather because you want to receive a reward or avoid punishment. This is the opposite of intrinsic motivation.

If not being sick is the goal, we need to focus on being fit, well & healthy.

Not being sick does not make someone healthier.

However, Western (allopathic) medicine and modern science have already proven that being in better mental and physical health usually helps the body's innate (natural) immunity to combat illness, disease and injuries.

It really is that simple. Our health, good or bad, is the manifestation of our lifestyle. What we eat, what we think and how we move our bodies - all our reflected in our well-being. Our health is ultimately our own individual responsibility. Obviously, some people's individual situation requires help and/or assistance from within our society. Socioeconomic issues affect many. But mostly, people have choices in the US regarding their own lifestyle and how it affects their own health. People usually are not forced to eat low-nutritional junk food, smoke or live a sedentary lifestyle. We make our own decisions and live with the causes, effects and results of our choices.

Cause

"Normal" in the US

- 12.2% of adults meet the
daily fruit intake recommendation
(CDC 2018)

- 9.3% of adults meet the daily
vegetable intake recommendation
(CDC 2018)

- 23% Exercise regularly (CDC 2018)

- 14% Smoke (CDC 2019)

www.MindAndBodyExercises.com

Effect

- 42% vitamin D deficiency (CDC 2018)

- 73% overweight (CDC 2018)

- 42% obese (CDC 2018)

- 18% obesity age 2-18 (CDC 2018)

- 70% on prescriptions (CDC 2019)

- 60% have chronic issues (CDC 2019)

- 40% have more than one chronic
issues (comorbidities) (CDC 2019)

www.MindAndBodyExercises.com

From the CDC (Center for Disease Control):

Chronic Diseases: Often Preventable, Frequently Manageable Many chronic diseases could be prevented, delayed, or alleviated, through simple lifestyle changes. The U.S. Centers for Disease Control and Prevention (CDC) estimates that eliminating three risk factors – poor diet, inactivity, and smoking – would prevent: 80% of heart disease and stroke; 80% of type 2 diabetes; and 40% of cancer.

Obesity steals more years than diabetes, tobacco, high blood pressure and high cholesterol -- the other top preventable health problems that cut Americans' lives short, according to researchers who analyzed 2014 data.

Pain is inevitable. Suffering is an option.

It is often very difficult to live a comfortable life, when someone has so much pain and suffering within it.

The keys to happiness are truly in our own hands. Self-discipline is the master key to do what we know needs to be done:

- maintain a nutritional diet

- consistently exercise and/or be active- prioritize sleep quality

- nurture healthy social interactions

- get fresh air and some sunlight every day

- be more positive than negative in your outlook and input

Result

Leading Causes of Death
(most preventable through lifestyle)

1) Heart disease: 690,882
2) Cancer: 598,932
3) Medical errors: 250,000-444,000
   (John Hopkins 2016)
3) COVID-19: 345,323
3) Accidents (unintentional injuries): 192,176
4) Chronic lower respiratory diseases: 151,637
5) Stroke (cerebrovascular diseases): 159,050
6) Alzheimer's disease: 133,382
7) Diabetes: 101,106
8) Kidney diseased: 52,260
9) Influenza and pneumonia: 53,495
10) Intentional self-harm (suicide): 44,834
Source: CDC 2020

www.MindAndBodyExercises.com

Highest Preventable Risk Factors
1) Poor diet
2) Inactivity
3) Smoking

Things You Can Manage

Food & Diet

Exercise

Sleep

Personal Responsibility

Stress Management

Relationships

www.MindAndBodyExercises.com

It Really is That Simple

What you spend time thinking about directly affects your mental and physical well-being!

It really is that simple:
- You can control your thoughts
- Your thoughts change your blood chemistry
- Your blood chemistry affects your internal organs
- The condition of your organs determines the quality & length of your life

---

Making Time to Exercise

We don't find time to exercise or do tasks we don't thoroughly enjoy doing. Rather we "make time" to enjoy the activities we see the benefit in performing.

We often don't enjoy cooking but enjoy the flavors, nourishment and sometimes camaraderie that come after the meal prep. Cleaning the house is no fun, but we appreciate not having junk or garbage staying in the house. You get the idea.

Many times, we don't enjoy the process of exercising but understand that benefits that follow. For some people, the preparation and time spent getting to the gym, club or studio seems to outweigh the return on investment. Many feel the need to look a certain way or dress in "exercise clothes" and travel to where they can exercise. This can be a lot of work and some expense before even starting the physical exercises to stay healthy.

Think about maybe cutting straight to the task and exercise right in your home, patio, or yard. It really is that simple. And you can get a cardio, aerobic or anaerobic, strength, flexibility, balance, and stress relieving session in minutes instead of hours. Exercise smarter, not harder.

https://youtu.be/fU3Pk6ctPzE

Managing the Inner Dialogue

We have an inner mental dialogue going on inside our head that mostly never stops. Often referred to as self-talk, inner chatter and inner speech. The next time you have disturbing thoughts or emotions, remember that it does not define or control you. After all, *you are not your thoughts* but rather the observer to your thoughts. You can actively choose whether to participate in it or not.

Whatever thoughts or feelings that happen to present themselves in your head at any given moment do not define or control you. You are not angry but rather can experience anger. We are not happy nor angry human beings but rather can choose to be happy, angry or whatever emotional state we care to experience at any given time. However, managing or controlling thoughts and consequently emotions is for most people not an easy task to achieve.

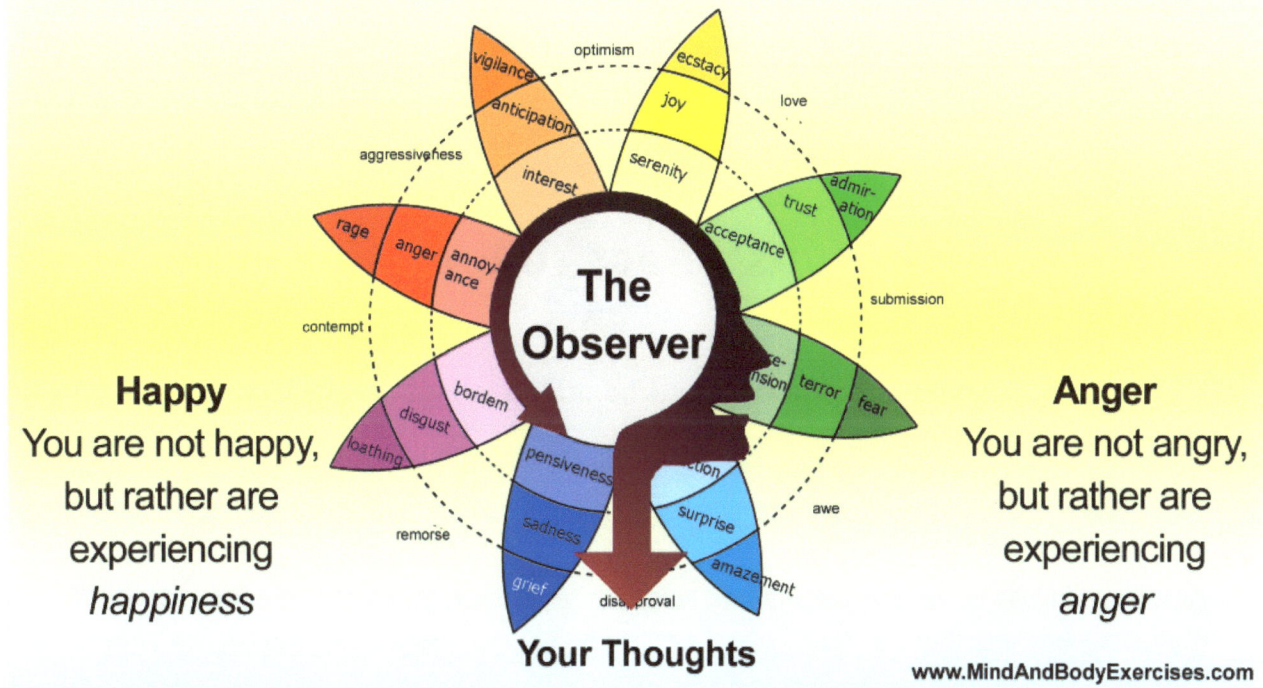

Become aware that you are not your thoughts

The Observer

Your Thoughts

Happy
You are not happy, but rather are experiencing *happiness*

Anger
You are not angry, but rather are experiencing *anger*

www.MindAndBodyExercises.com

Thoughts Affect Your Emotions

Every thought has an emotional attachment on some level. Positive emotions keep organs in balance for optimal performance. Negative emotions disrupt this balance leading to other symptoms and ailments.

Thoughts affect your emotions

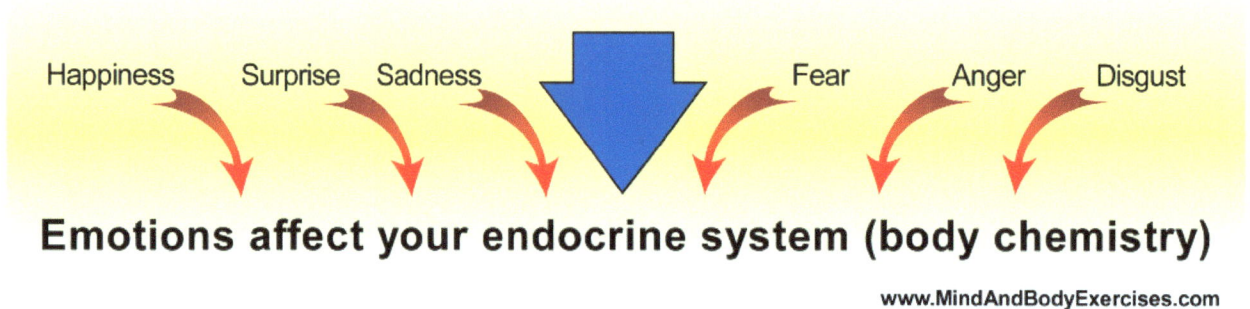

Happiness   Surprise   Sadness   Fear   Anger   Disgust

Emotions affect your endocrine system (body chemistry)

- Emotions affect the endocrine system (body chemistry)

- The body chemistry affects hormones (growth & stress)

- Growth or stress hormones affect bodily functions of the physical health

- Physical health affects your thoughts - completing the circuit brings us back full circle

Thoughts Affect Your Health

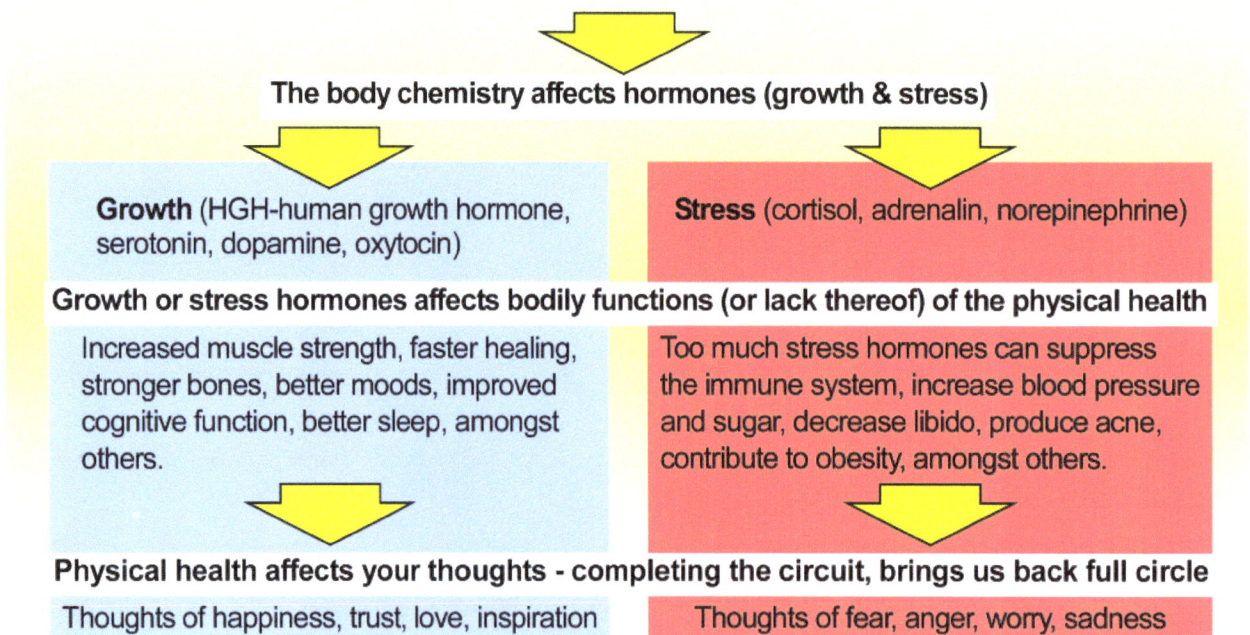

The body chemistry affects hormones (growth & stress)

Growth (HGH-human growth hormone, serotonin, dopamine, oxytocin)

Stress (cortisol, adrenalin, norepinephrine)

Growth or stress hormones affects bodily functions (or lack thereof) of the physical health

Increased muscle strength, faster healing, stronger bones, better moods, improved cognitive function, better sleep, amongst others.

Too much stress hormones can suppress the immune system, increase blood pressure and sugar, decrease libido, produce acne, contribute to obesity, amongst others.

Physical health affects your thoughts - completing the circuit, brings us back full circle

Thoughts of happiness, trust, love, inspiration

Thoughts of fear, anger, worry, sadness

What You Think Affects Your Outlook

If your thoughts have a mostly positive emotional attachment on some level, you may have more of an optimistic outlook in your life. Conversely, mostly negative emotions tend to make people have a somewhat pessimistic outlook in their life.

Thoughts Affect Your Organs

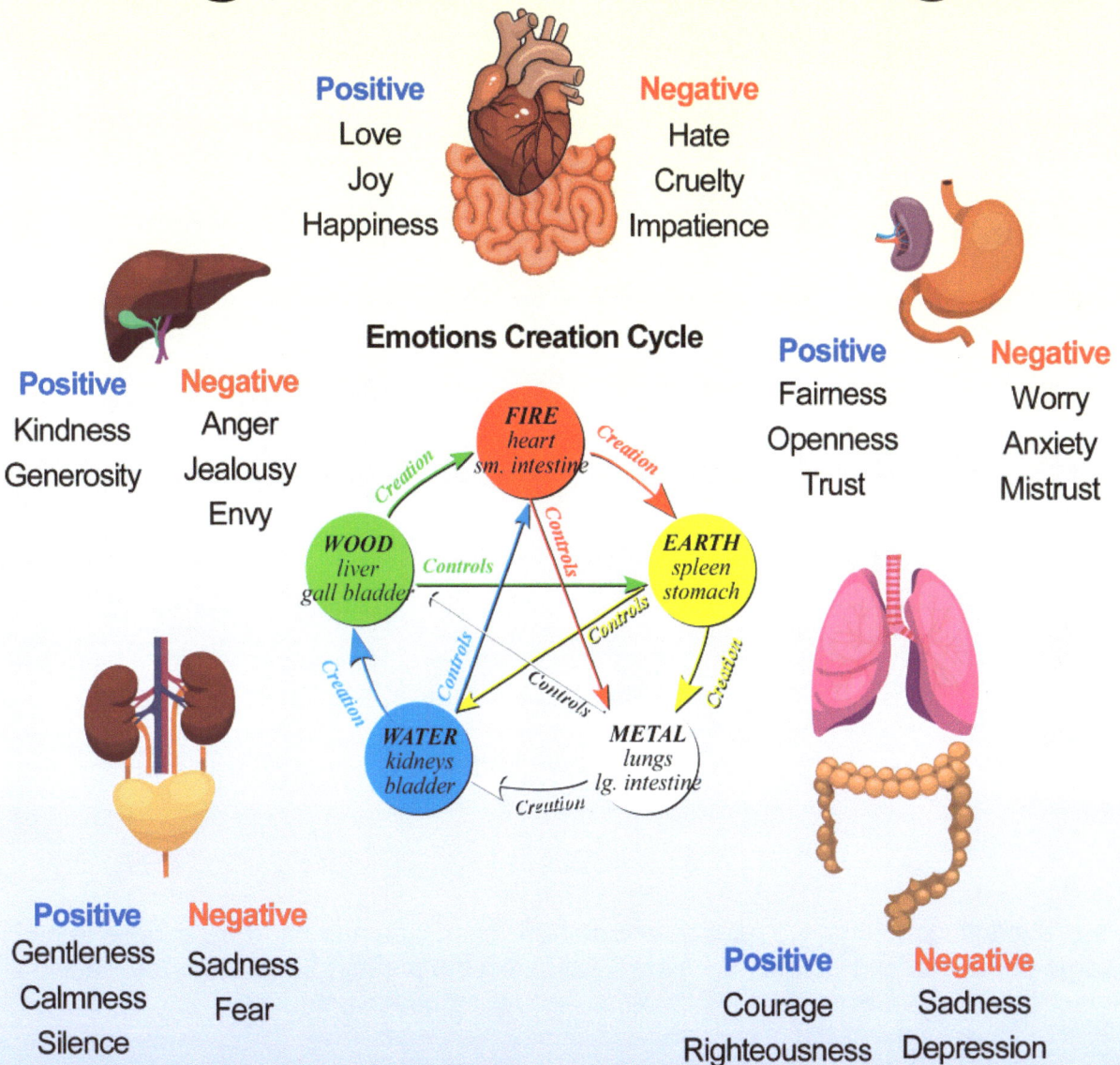

Positive
Love
Joy
Happiness

Negative
Hate
Cruelty
Impatience

Positive
Kindness
Generosity

Negative
Anger
Jealousy
Envy

Positive
Fairness
Openness
Trust

Negative
Worry
Anxiety
Mistrust

Emotions Creation Cycle

FIRE
heart
sm. intestine

WOOD
liver
gall bladder

EARTH
spleen
stomach

WATER
kidneys
bladder

METAL
lungs
lg. intestine

Creation

Controls

Positive
Gentleness
Calmness
Silence

Negative
Sadness
Fear

Positive
Courage
Righteousness

Negative
Sadness
Depression

Traditional Chinese Medicine recognizes that there is a direct link from our emotions to the health of our internal organs and their functions.

21

Tai chi, yoga, martial arts, meditation and other time-proven methods are known practices to help manage and control the inner dialogue.

A recent article from the Wall Street Journal explains more about managing the inner chatter.

https://www.wsj.com/articles/how-to-stop-the-negative-chatter-in-your-head-11609876801?page=1

As we all continue to age, we need to decide how much time and effort we choose to put towards our health and well-being. Weekly hours of time pursuing a healthy lifestyle can prevent potential hours at the doctor's office or days in the hospital.

Mindfulness Used to be Called "Paying attention"

Years back, mindfulness was called paying attention.

Some smart marketers decided that "paying attention" could be re-branded into "mindfulness" and a billion-dollar industry was created. Seminars, retreats, classes, phone apps and a plethora of other events and items have come about to help people learn to pay attention or be more mindful.

However, Eastern philosophy and its methods of yoga (qigong), tai chi and others, have been around for thousands of years and have already been proven to improve mental and physical health. Better fitness, health and well-being usually help the body's innate (natural) immunity to combat illness, disease and injuries.

Mind, Body & Spirit. Many people talk about this but how do you actually be more present. Watch my video below of my introductory Tai Chi & Qigong class at the University Club of Winter Park to learn how these methods help us to pay better attention to what is most important in our lives.

Physical Exercise (body)

Regulated Breathing (mind)

Self-Awareness (spirit)

The former are key components to a healthy lifestyle. However, more important is the **quality or specificity** of how you exercise for your abilities and limitations. **How deep and the frequency** of your breaths is more important than just being able to breathe. What you think about determines the **quality of your thoughts** being positive or negative with both affecting the emotions and consequently the nervous system and blood chemistry.

It really is that simple. Our health, good or bad, is the manifestation of our lifestyle. What we eat, what we think and how we move our bodies - all our reflected in our well-being. Our health is ultimately our own individual responsibility. Obviously, some people's individual situation requires help and/or assistance from within our society. Socioeconomic issues affect many. But mostly, people have choices in the US regarding their own lifestyle and how it affects their own health. People usually are not forced to eat low-nutritional junk food, smoke or live a sedentary lifestyle. We make our own decisions and live with the causes, effects and results of our choices.

https://youtu.be/f2ekJxv4Rik

Never Stop Learning

Martial arts have so many facets that many people are unaware of. Having been around this learning environment for almost 40 years, I realize that there is such a wide spectrum of theories, techniques, methods, etc. that are more vast than what can be covered in one lifetime.

I spend part of almost every day journaling and graphically representing much of what I have come to understand with the hope that others can gain us much as I have from my teachers, mentors and peers.

New Year's Commitments

Start a New Year's tradition by stopping the usual New Year's resolution shenanigans, which usually last a day, a week or maybe a month. Take accountability to take care of yourself mentally and physically.

If you are not striving to grow as a human being every day, you are consequently dying a little bit every day. Nature and our world within it, is constantly changing, evolving and moving forward. If we are not moving forward within this flow, we are not just stuck in place but rather falling behind.

Well then, Happy New Year!

If you are not growing, then you're dying.

Start a new tradition by stopping the usual New Year's resolution shenanigans, which usually are seldom kept or maybe at best last a day, a week or maybe a month until they are revisited another year later.

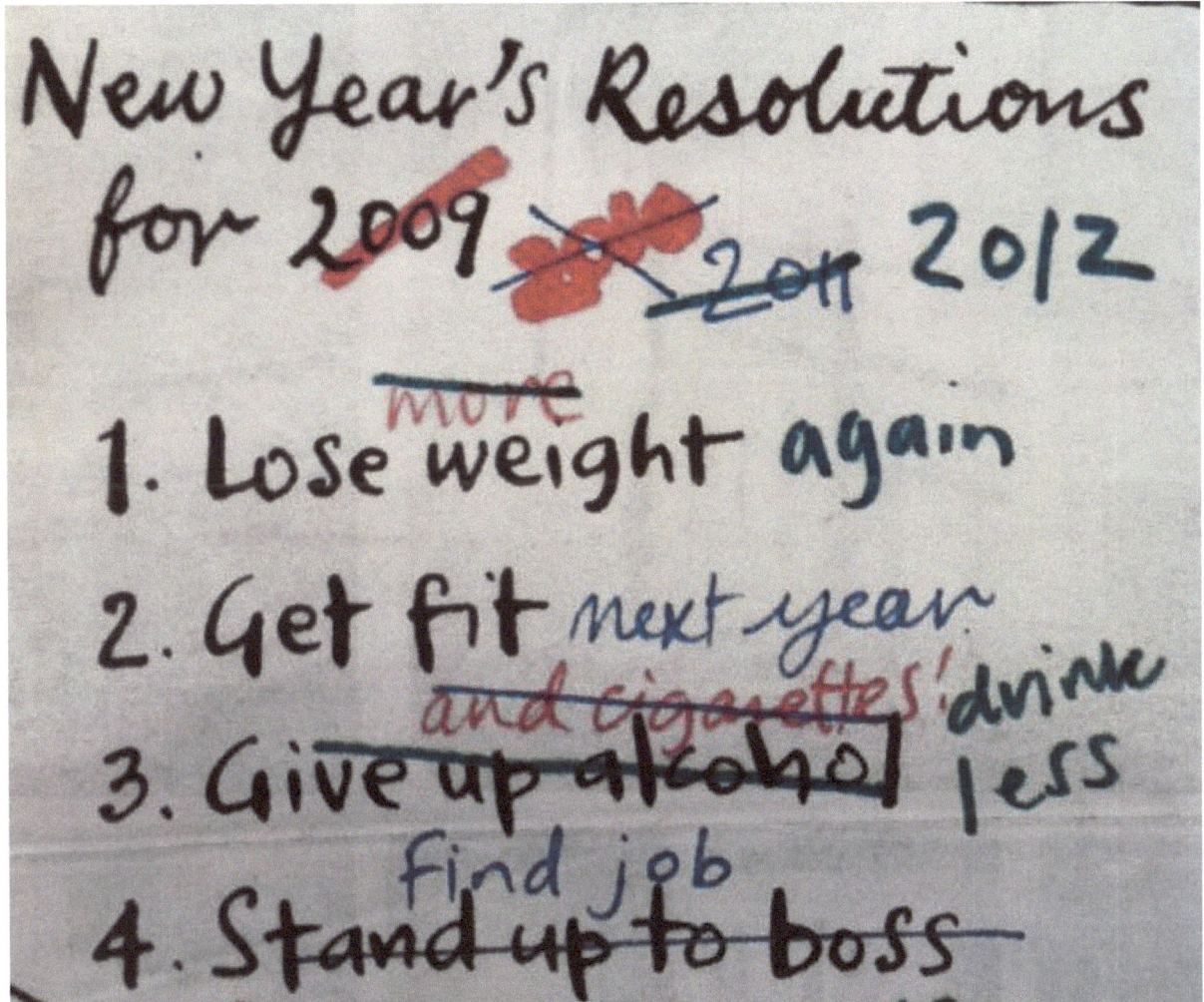

The vicious cycle continues and often never changes, because there is no accountability to take care of yourself mentally, physically, and spiritually. And often there is a loss of proper motivation - until the spark arrives. An illness, an injury, or an event that enlightens us to what is truly important. Then this spark motivates us to pursue better methods to maintain our mind, body and spiritual awareness.

25

New Year's Resolutions
How often are they kept?

January 1

Every year, millions of Americans make New Year's resolutions...

→

By February, 80% of them have failed.

What gives?

According to psychology experts, the only way to start checking off your goals is to change your own level of motivation.

https://elcidonline.com/features/2017/12/21/coming-to-fruition-or-not/

How someone behaves when there is no audience or opportunity to gain is more of a gauge of an individual's moral compass. Changing one's behavior when in the presence of family, friends and others can be somewhat manageable, and truly just a facade for many people. Do you really care about your health and well-being, and reflect this in your daily actions or just parrot the words of others encouraging "be healthy, stay safe"? No one should care more about your health and well-being than you, right?

Instead of another face value New Year's Resolution, this year seriously consider making a REAL promise or commitment to yourself to improve or maintain a healthy lifestyle. Eat healthier, be more active, sleep better, be more positive than negative in your outlook - live a purposeful life without fear.

People are afraid to die, and even more afraid to live

Sylvia Browne

Tai chi, qigong, wellness classes and lectures might be options in your future. Holistic health classes may offer a diverse knowledge base covering the following aspects:

- Anatomy and physiology
- Body mechanics
- Wellness concepts
- Learning concepts
- Stress management
- Chronic pain management
- Physical rehabilitation
- Functionally specific exercise sets
- Self-awareness
- Traditional Chinese Medicine
- Eastern philosophy
- Sound Therapy
- Various meditation methods

For at least the last few decades, we have known that in order to maintain wellness we need a healthy mind, body and spirit. The state of our health directly impacts our body's innate (natural) immunity against disease, illness and injury.

Eat quality food, be active, avoid stress, sleep soundly, drink alcohol responsibility, don't smoke, maintain positive relationships, enjoy life - these are known and science-proven components to maintain wellness. Why did these concepts lose popularity and credibility?

For whatever reason, our society for the last year and half, has pretty much disconnected the key components of health, fitness and wellness from personal responsibility. We have grown accustomed to blaming somebody, anybody, and everybody for our health issues, when we ultimately make the decisions of what we put into our bodies and the lifestyle we live.

Obviously not everyone's socioeconomic situation allows for the Utopia of the perfect society many seek. But overall, our US citizens possess the freedom and ability to change the exact things that make us sick and dis-"ease"d.

"Normal" in the US:

- 12.2% of adults meet the daily fruit intake recommendation (CDC 2018)

- 9.3% of adults meet the daily vegetable intake recommendation (CDC 2018)

- 23% Exercise regularly (CDC 2018)

- 42% vitamin D deficiency (CDC 2018)

- 73% overweight (CDC 2018)

- 42% obese (CDC 2018)

- 18% obesity age 2-18 (CDC 2018)

- 70% on prescriptions (CDC 2019)

- 60% have chronic issues (CDC 2019)

- 40% have more than one chronic issue (comorbidities) (CDC 2019)

- 14% Smoke (CDC 2019)

These are the reasons why the US spends the most $$$ of all nations on healthcare but does not even rank in the top 30 nations for quality of life.

I am adamantly pursuing opportunities to share and teach methods of mind, body and self-awareness to open and willing health-conscious individuals. I teach and encourage people how to live a healthy lifestyle. Learn how this works and relates to your health and well-being.

https://youtu.be/sHWu5BRAm3c

_____

No one should prioritize your health and well-being more than you.

Breaking It Down:

Personal Ownership: Your health is uniquely experienced by you. Others may empathize, but only you endure the consequences of poor diet, stress, inactivity, or illness. Recognizing this positions you as the primary agent of your well-being.

Self-Advocacy: In areas such as medical care, fitness, or mental health, it is essential to actively pursue optimal solutions for yourself. This involves researching, asking pertinent questions, and making informed decisions rather than relying passively on others to dictate your well-being.

Daily Choices Matter: No one else can control your dietary habits, physical activity, sleep quality, or stress management. These routine decisions cumulatively impact your overall health over time.

Limits of External Care: Healthcare practitioners possess knowledge and expertise but have limited patient interaction time. Similarly, loved ones may care deeply but have their own responsibilities. Sole reliance on external sources for your well-being may result in neglect or mismanagement.

Mind-Body Connection: Comprehensive wellness encompasses not only physical health but also mental and emotional balance. Prioritizing oneself involves engaging in self-care practices that nurture all facets of your being.

Deeply caring about your own health is not an act of selfishness but a necessity. Taking ownership establishes a robust foundation for longevity, vitality, and overall life satisfaction. While others can offer support and guidance, ultimately, **your health lies in your hands**.

Science, Where to Follow What Fits Our Viewpoints

Coffee is bad for you, but studies show that it might be good for you.

Cow's milk is good for humans, unless you read the studies that say it is not so much. Moderate alcohol consumption is good for you, unless you find the medical studies that say it is not.

Sun exposure is bad for the skin, but good for vitamin D production, immunity and bone health, until one develops skin cancer.

Cigarette smoking was at one time recommended by doctors to help promote health and relieve stress.

The list goes on and on. Which "science" do we choose to believe? Well, whichever science that supports our own individual beliefs, viewpoints and agendas. Maybe the truth of the science lies in that all things are relative, yin and yang in all things for those that understand that life is constantly changing and often there are no absolutes. Maybe all of the above are good in moderation, but not so much when in excess or abuse.

Trust in science alone may make people more susceptible to pseudoscience. Science literacy & critical thinking are crucial.

Media and science…kind of like oil and water. I feel these days, that media reports on what they feel the American public should know. News outlets use to be somewhat neutral. Currently, most don't even try to be neutral but rather tout what direction their reports lean towards. Fox News, Prager U and others, makes no qualms about being quite to the right, whereas CNN, MSNBC and New York Times reports leaning quite to the left. So, who should and shouldn't report on what leads us to 1st amendment discussions about who determines what is truth and misinformation. Seems like there are now multiple truths these days depending upon the source and the agenda in play. Universal truths that everyone can agree upon, like water is wet, the sun rises in the east and that humans are mortals will still be debated given an audience and someone willing to debate these facts.

What is true for everyone (not your truth or my truth silliness) is that we need to be more active, eat healthier, sleep better, stress less, develop self-discipline. These are the key components to maintaining a strong mind, body, immune system, and outlook on life.

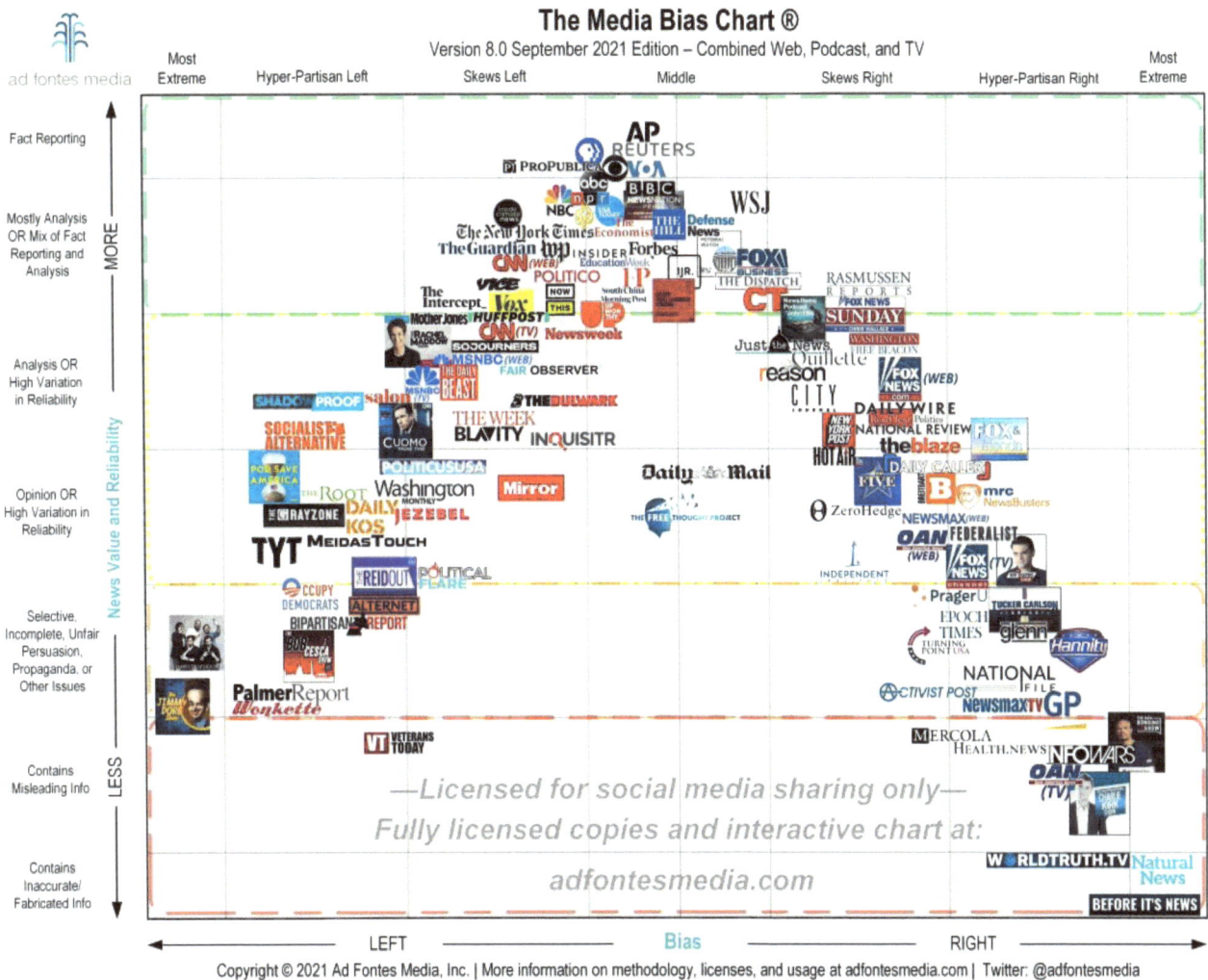

The Media Bias Chart ®
Version 8.0 September 2021 Edition – Combined Web, Podcast, and TV

Self-awareness Can be Developed

How aware are you of seeing yourself for who you truly are? Can you see every line, mark or feature on your face in your thoughts without looking in the mirror? If no one is around to see your actions, do you still keep your morals and values in check? Seeing yourself as others see you, and not caring what others think of you are two entirely different discussions. This post is about the ongoing cultivation of trying to become the best version of yourself and not about how to justify our poor behavior or actions towards those we interact with. Now then, how can we become more self-aware to be the best we can be?

SELF-CONTROL
Choosing to do what is right, when feeling like doing what is wrong.

I have found from my almost 40 years of studying, practicing and teaching martial arts and other Eastern wellness methods, that it is much easier to become aware of our physical body than to know how our mind works. Therefore, the body is the key to the mind. The mind controls the body. Our body protects our mind. We are not our thoughts, but rather the observer of our thoughts or consciousness. Our body doesn't move on its own, other than for reflexes and autonomic functions. Our body doesn't make the decisions to get up, open the refrigerator, and put something to eat in our mouth. Junk food or healthy snacks. You as the observer make these choices. Our thoughts do not make these decisions either, but rather our consciousness. Once one becomes self-aware of their consciousness, now they can observe their thoughts and choose to direct them with us without emotion. For example, after opening the refrigerator and accidentally dropping a glass container that shatters, we choose how to react to this maybe by experiencing regret, anger, frustration, sadness, etc. Or maybe you really didn't like that container to begin with and now you are happy, relieved or indifferent after all it was only a glass container and not your house catching on fire or someone being seriously injured.

Ship Pal Gye, Taoist yoga or the "Filling the 8 Vessels" are methods to increase the capacity of your nervous system. By holding the body in specific alignments, the nervous system is strengthened to endure more pain, stress and discomfort. Think of tempering steel in fire to strengthen the metal. Building self-discipline of the mind and body simultaneously!

When engaging the muscles, tendons, bones and fascia, the 12 regular energy meridians are engaged plus the 8 extraordinary meridians are opened and filled as reservoirs to adjust the ebb and flow of energy throughout the body and thereby strengthening the immune system among other bodily functions.

Exercise methods like these have been known for centuries but are considered new or "alternative" to modern western culture.

Often times people will ask me, "where did you learn this?" Well...almost 40 years ago I began studying Korean kung fu, then Traditional Chinese Medicine, medical qigong, fitness, wellness and anatomy. It didn't happen overnight or from a weekend seminar. It took me decades of learning, studying and teaching from and with high level masters and teachers. And I'm not done learning yet, are you?

You are not your thoughts!

For most people, it is very difficult to train or discipline their mind and consequently, their body. People often say or do things they regret only to realize later that they lacked the self-control and self-awareness to make good decisions to begin with. By gaining control of the physical anatomy, a relationship with the physical body is developed. Attention to the details of your body positioning is what trains the mind to become more self-aware. When aligning the limbs and joints to stretch and strengthen them, while also maintaining deep and deliberate breathing rhythms, an individual can cultivate a more harmonious link between the mind, body and spirit (self-awareness). Practice exercises that truly engage the mind and body, (very much like yoga, tai chi, isometrics) to improve health & wellness. The mind directs the body, while the body protects the mind.

Discipline the body by disciplining the mind
(attention to the details is what trains the mind to become more self-aware)

Opening the 9 Gates & Filling the 8 Vessels   www.MindAndBodyExercises.com

By holding specific postures, the musculoskeletal, nervous and other functional systems are engaged.

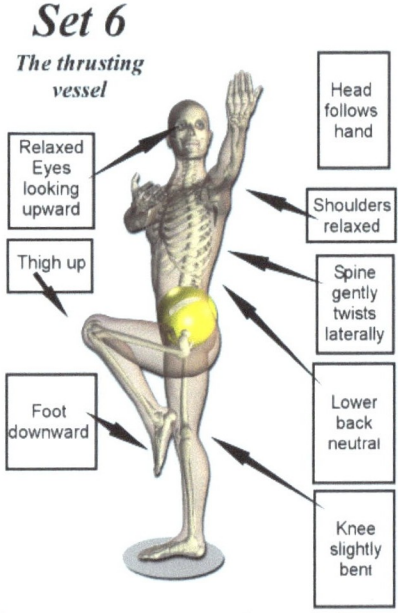

Set 6
The thrusting vessel

- Relaxed Eyes looking upward
- Thigh up
- Foot downward
- Head follows hand
- Shoulders relaxed
- Spine gently twists laterally
- Lower back neutral
- Knee slightly bent

Hold for: 30 seconds, 1-5 minutes, longer if advanced

Ship Pal Gye, Taoist yoga or the "Filling the 8 Vessels"

Few people exercise or stay active (only about 23% CDC 2018) let alone practice the physical and mental skills that can protect themselves or loved ones.

If You Have Never Had to Defend Yourself, Nor Practiced Self-defense - How Do You Know What You Will Do?

Typical Ways People Are Assaulted

Choke (front) — Choke (behind) — Double Shoulder (behind) — Double Shoulder (front) — Punch to Face

Same Side Wrist — Cross Side Wrist — Double Wrists (behind) — Double Wrists (front) — Sitting On Top

Bear Hug (behind) — Bear Hug (front) — Knife Lunge — Knife on Throat

Self-awareness & Self-defense are skills that can be practiced to improve success

www.MindAndBodyExercises.com

Kids don't play outside or together as much as they use to. Video games and smartphones are the substitute for physical activity and developing social skills. Both are needed to avoid physical confrontations. In reality, most kids (and adults) never learn how to defend themselves these days until after the actual need arises – which unfortunately could be too late.

We live in a very different world than when we did a few decades back. If you believe television and movies, everyone knows kung fu, boxing or mixed martial arts (MMA). However, this is not reality.

Good skills to learn:

- Basic defense skills against being grabbed, touched, punched, kicked, etc.

- Anatomy relative to "pressure points" or key body parts to defend or attack if necessary.

- Situational awareness relative to options before and after someone finds themselves in a potentially dangerous and life changing event.

- Balance, coordination and strength exercises to develop self-esteem and confidence that one does not need to be a victim or rely upon others for their own personal safety.

Stand Here, No Here, Over There, Not Here...

The quest continues to pursue a return to "normal" in spite of the ever-changing facts of science and how we adjust our actions in response. There is plenty of blame to go around, red, blue, green, yellow - pick your favorite color of the rainbow to blame. However, while blame may satisfy our ego in determining whose fault this all is, blame does not fix our problems. Our own actions of personal self-care through self-responsibility are the key to our better health and happiness.

The root causes of our public healthcare hesitancy come from a growing distrust of our government and medical experts that often never seem to agree on any course of action and what fact or science is. I think there will always be opposition to government intervention, depending upon the issue and who it affects the most. However, in the case of the current pandemic, the distrust has grown seemingly across many demographics. In my humble opinion, I think there have been numerous times when government leaders (politicians and medical experts) stated a particular direction and then soon after changed that course. When this continued to happen over the last 2 years, the public trust eroded rapidly to where we are today.

Figure 1. Timeline of COVID-19 in the United States. CDC: Centers for Disease Control and Prevention; FDA: Food and Drug Administration.

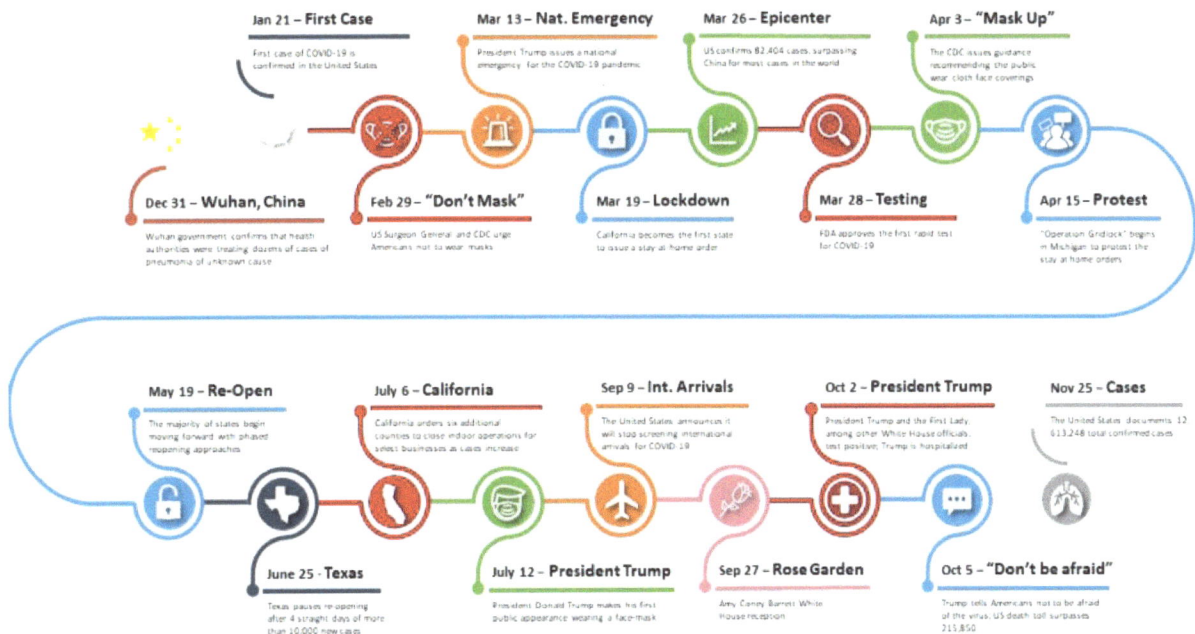

- In late 2019, government leaders said the US was fine and had no worries with the Covid19 virus, as it was contained in China. People were encouraged to enjoy the holidays and not be afraid. Obviously, it was not contained and Covid19 made its way to the US in early 2020 and probably even earlier in late 2019.
- Shutting down the US borders in early 2020, in response to Covid19, was considered xenophobic. Late in 2021, the US restricted foreign traveler's entry due to the Omicron variant and xenophobia was barely mentioned by leaders and news outlets.
- Similarly, early in 2020 theories of a possible virus leak from the Wuhan Institute of Virology were seen as racist, xenophobic and the product of conspiracy fanatics. Later in 2020, some US leaders and the World Health Organization were supporting investigation of the Wuhan lab, albeit a day late and a dollar short.
- In early 2020 Americans were directed by the government and medical experts to lock-down at home for 2 weeks to "flatten the curve", referring to the spike in cases hopefully leveling off with a relatively short amount of time. Instead, lock-downs continued in some areas, off and on for the next 12 months.
- In December of 2020, then president elect Joe Biden stated if he became president that he would not mandate Covid19 vaccination mandates. In early September of 2021 President Biden mandated vaccines for all businesses of 100 or more employees.
- The CDC has changed its direction numerous times on masking, distancing, quarantine duration and other relative information. As scientific data changed, so did the CDC's confusing guidance on quarantining from 10 days to 5 days. However, this change was implemented during a massive increase in infections of the Omicron variant during the end of 2021. More infections nationwide, but less quarantine time led many people to believe the changes were more politically motivated and not science-based, in order to keep people working in healthcare, retail, etc. to maintain

the economy through the holidays and coming winter months where many other illnesses often flourish.

Understanding that science is a process and not a belief system can help us to better understand that science is an evolving process of research, discovery and conclusions - that will all continue to change as time proceeds forward.

What is Science

- **Science** is a continuous stream of ideas that are constantly being reshaped, added to, subtracted from and built upon.
- **Science** is always evolving and changing!
- **Science** is about predictability! It gives us the ability to predict certain things about the world around us.

Science is always evolving and changing! Science is about predictability! It gives us the ability to predict certain things about the world around us.

People do pay attention to what government leaders say and often try to hold them to their words. Continuously changing information and direction, if not distributed consistently and with transparency, leads to more distrust. I think that it will be very difficult for the US government and medical experts to regain the trust of the American people any time soon. If there was perhaps some transparency, sense of humility or humility by leaders, confirming that they really don't know exactly how to handle our national (and worldwide) crisis, but that they are doing their best and have a way yet to go, it would maybe instill some level of hope in people.

How to Think Like a Scientist

- **Be Curious-** look around and ask questions.
- **Be Skeptical-** Don't always believe the first thing you hear or read.
- **Be Flexible-** Even if you have found one explanation, look for another one.
- These three brain exercises add up to what is called **Critical Thinking**.

Be Curious- look around and ask questions. Be Skeptical- Don't always believe the first thing you hear or read. Be Flexible- Even if you have found one explanation, look for another one. These three brain exercises add up to what is called Critical Thinking.

Regardless of vaccination status, social distancing and masking for the greater good, other lifestyle vices too have a ripple effect on our healthcare system & personal well-being. If a poor diet, smoking, being stressed all day, drug/alcohol abuse, being overweight/obese, etc. only affects that person, realize that the whole healthcare system takes a hit for these "bad behaviors" as well . This puts a strain on the whole system causing inefficiency due to the sheer numbers of ill people or by issues impacting others around you through stress, money, time & other resources. Those relying solely on pharmaceuticals to stay sick-free, still should eat healthier, be active, get sunlight & fresh air, stop smoking, manage stress - in other words "build their natural immunity". Shouldn't natural immunity through living a healthier lifestyle be promoted to keep the next virus or pathogen at bay? The top causes of death in the US (cancer, heart & lung disease) and root causes can often be managed through lifestyle choices. Scientific data has proven that the majority of deaths related to Covid19 are from people who had multiple comorbidities, exacerbating death not from Covid19 but rather death with Covid19. More than 81% of COVID-19 related deaths occur in people over 65. The number of deaths among people over age 65 is 80 times higher than the number of deaths among people aged 18-29.

How to Act Like a Scientist

The Scientific Method

- **Observation-** Careful watching of something around us.
- **Hypothesis-** An educated guess explaining what you are observing or how to change what you are observing.
- **Experiment-** Testing your hypothesis by designing and carrying out an experiment.

The Scientific Method. Observation- Careful watching of something around us. Hypothesis- An educated guess explaining what you are observing or how to change what you are observing. Experiment- Testing your hypothesis by designing and carrying out an experiment.

Maybe it's time for us to reevaluate what normal is and choose to not go back to it, but rather move towards healthier, smarter, wiser.

Harvard Medical School - recommends taking care of your immune system. Stay healthy by living healthy. Masks and social distancing don't make someone healthy if their habits are not healthy to begin with. Take the steps before you get ill.

https://www.health.harvard.edu/diseases-and-conditions/preventing-the-spread-of-the-coronavirus#:~:text=%2D%20Don't%20smoke,nose%2C%20and%20mouth.

What can I do to keep my immune system strong?

Your immune system is your body's defense system. When a harmful invader — like a cold or flu virus, or the coronavirus that causes COVID-19 — gets into your body, your immune system mounts an attack. Known as an immune response, this attack is a sequence of events that involves various cells and unfolds over time.

Following general health guidelines is the best step you can take toward keeping your immune system strong and healthy. Every part of your body, including your immune system, functions better when protected from environmental assaults and bolstered by healthy-living strategies such as these:

- Don't smoke or vape.
- Eat a diet high in fruits, vegetables, and whole grains.
- Take a multivitamin if you suspect that you may not be getting all the nutrients you need through your diet.
- Exercise regularly.
- Maintain a healthy weight.
- Control your stress level.
- Control your blood pressure.
- If you drink alcohol, drink only in moderation (no more than one to two drinks a day for men, no more than one a day for women).
- Get enough sleep.
- Take steps to avoid infection, such as washing your hands frequently and trying not to touch your hands to your face, since harmful germs can enter through your eyes, nose, and mouth.

41

Strive to have a "relationship with your physical body".

I think often people hear about the mind, body and spirit connection but really have no idea, plan or methods on how to achieve this state of being.

From what I have learned from my teachers of martial arts & qigong is that by becoming aware and understanding how the physical body exists and operates (kind of from a mechanical or physiological perspective) one can begin to better understand how one's own mind works. For example, if holding a particular yoga, qigong or kung fu posture for say 1-5 minutes, the muscles and the physical body begin to fatigue. The process of the mind trying to keep the body in the correct position engages the thoughts to express emotional traits of patience, frustration, determination, focus and other levels of awareness. This can also be similarly developed from other mind/body practices such as archery, painting, singing, playing an instrument, carpentry or other trades that all require repetitive engagement of the thought process and the control of the body to accomplish a particular task. These types of activities can be viewed as various types of sitting, standing, or moving meditations all in their own rights.

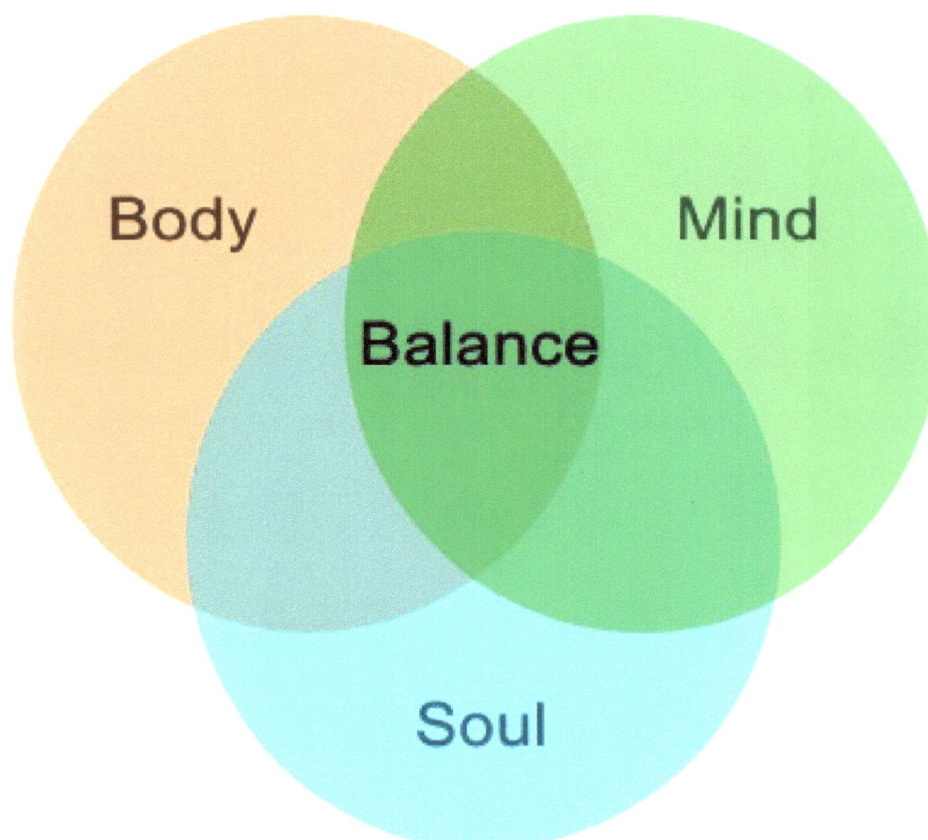

Background music can be a pro or con depending upon the goal of the practitioner. Some martial arts or dance styles utilize drums to keep a beat that coincides with the pace of the movements. Others moving meditations like tai chi or qigong might incorporate music that consists of specific tones or tempos to help to coincide the breathing and heart rates to slower paces, thereby hacking the parasympathetic nervous system and reducing stress. Certain tones can either help elevate the heart rate (like maybe Led Zeppelin) while others might lower the heart rate (maybe jazz or instrumentals), where as in TCM specific notes are associated with wood (liver-gall bladder), fire (heart-small intestines), earth (stomach-spleen), metal (lungs-large intestine) and water (bladder-kidneys).

The Gradual Decline of Physical Education in Schools & Relevance to Adult Health

I thought I'd share my perspective on this subject of state of American health. Mostly just my opinion from my experiences as a father of 2 young adults and teacher (martial arts, wellness, qigong, Taoist yoga etc.) for almost 40 years. Yes, I am showing my age. When I was in elementary school in the 70's, we had a 1/2-hour recess and 1-hour of physical education (PE) every school day. Middle & high school was PE everyday regardless of weather. I cannot remember more than 1-2 kids during that time as being labeled "hyperactive" however a lot more kids had trouble focusing and getting good grades in particular subjects; so focus had always been an issue on some level. Ritalin was the only medicine that I had even known to exist for a few young people, that had what was to in later decades diagnosed as ADHD.

Active Students = Better Learners
www.cdc.gov/healthyschools/PEandPA

43

Fast forward to the last 20 years of my life. My kids while in elementary school had recess for about 15-20 minutes a few days a week alternating with PE for two days a week. High school required 1 credit of PE over the 4 years of attendance; online or in person were the options. Talking with other parents and teachers over this time led me to understand that a large portion of kids were having ADHD, depression, anxiety, obesity and many other health issues that were dealt with through pharmaceuticals on a daily basis. Sports and PE were often not even considered as methods to manage these ailments. Getting good grades and into a good college are the main focus in high school, leaving little time for such non-academic pursuits of physical activities that actually make the mind work better.

Having discussed this issue with many schoolteachers that I knew as friends, most felt that less recess and PE was a major step backwards in child development. Additionally, these teachers felt that it was much more difficult for them to teach while attempting to harness the pent-up energy and emotions of kids sitting for hours on end throughout the school day. Most wished that recess and PE were brought back as a standard daily requirement.

So, I strongly believe that yoga and other mindful methods would be great (this is what I teach!) I would be very happy just to see regular exercise of running, swimming, calisthenics, and game play come back to all levels of school. So many benefits for the mind and body that are associated with whatever level of physical as well as mental and social engagement that are being left out of schools in lieu of more time spent on academics. If we are to have a strong and healthy population, we really need to plant seeds of good health education and self-responsibility with our youth, in order to make it grow into the adult years.

Welcome to Your New Part-time Job - Your Health!

As we all continue to age, we need to decide how much time and effort we choose to put towards our health and well being. Weekly hours of time pursuing a healthy lifestyle can prevent potential hours at the doctor's office or days in the hospital.

Self-care

- relies mostly on the individual taking preventative and proactive methods to maintain a healthy lifestyle.

Healthcare

- relies mostly on the individual seeking medical professionals to maintain a lifestyle free from illness and discomfort.

The Health Care Crisis & Personal Responsibility

If every person in American spent 5 minutes (or more) every day by exercising, more people could better manage their weight and suffer less from related illnesses.

If every person in American spent 5 minutes (or more) every day calming their mind by practicing deep breathing exercises, more people would be less stressed and suffer less from related illnesses.

If every person in American spent every day becoming more conscious of their nutrition habits, more people would be able to maintain their health through the choices they make while eating and drinking and suffer less from related illnesses.

If everyone could assume personal responsibility for their own health, our nation would not have to spend as much time, effort, energy and money trying to keep people healthy.

These concepts seem easy enough, but in reality, most people lack the desire or self-discipline to make the effort and do what it takes to stay healthy, prevent illness or cure their own ailments. Self-discipline is one of five steps known to help achieve better mental and physical wellness.

1) Respect – This is where values begin. You must understand and have respect for yourself (self-respect) before you can demonstrate it to others. Taking the steps to take care of your physical and mental well-being affects you first and then those closest to you second.

2) Discipline – Developing control of one's own desires, commitments, and ultimately your own actions, leads to self-discipline. Control of physical exercises can lead to management of thought and emotion.

3) Self-Esteem – As you review your achievements of respect and discipline, your sense of worth is elevated and appreciated.

4) Confidence – Understanding and accepting your weak areas as well as your stronger aspects removes insecurity. When you feel that you are physically well and mentally sharp, confidence can fill your personality. You can accomplish whatever goal you set out to achieve.

5) Determination to Achieve Goals – The positive sum of the previous aspects leads to one's determination. Good judgment and focused effort toward positive goals result in true personal success.

Qigong, Tai Chi and Yoga all are methods to achieve these traits.

It doesn't matter so much that you do these exercises, as much as it matters that you do some type of exercise. Walk, jog, swim or whatever - just get going and do something. 5 minutes here and there can quickly turn into 15 or 30 minutes at one time or over the course of a day. Once you are moving or mentally engaged, it is much easier to stay motivated and try a few more exercises for a few more minutes.

The New Healthcare Program is Actually the Old Program - Self-care

Get your body moving, breathe deep and engage your mind.

A time-proven curriculum
A teacher willing to share.
A community for support and contrast.

My goal is to present an education that brings awareness to these time-proven methods. With an intent to de-mystify and simplify explanations, hopefully more people can come to realize that we are all accountable for our own well-being.

https://youtu.be/X1Bu_AUxGCQ

Time to Avoid Excuses in Your Life

Currently, many of us seem to have a lot of extra time on our hands. But we often talk to ourselves about doing things we know need to be done. It is that way. Part of being human is being lazy.

Come on let's face it, we do often try to find the route of least resistance. We sit when we can stand. We drive when we can walk. We take the elevator instead of the stairs. Some even complain they have no time to take care of themselves but can find time to watch television and check their smartphone throughout the whole day.

My solution to this part of the human condition, is to take baby steps. That's it! A minute or two, here and there add up throughout your day. Once you get moving it seems easier to keep moving for a while longer.

Sir Isaac Newton proposed his First Law of Motion, the law of inertia, in 1687: A body at rest tends to remain at rest. A body in motion tends to stay in motion. Bodies will continue in their current state, whether at rest or in motion, unless acted on by a greater outside force.

https://youtu.be/wbfZjfCj-MY

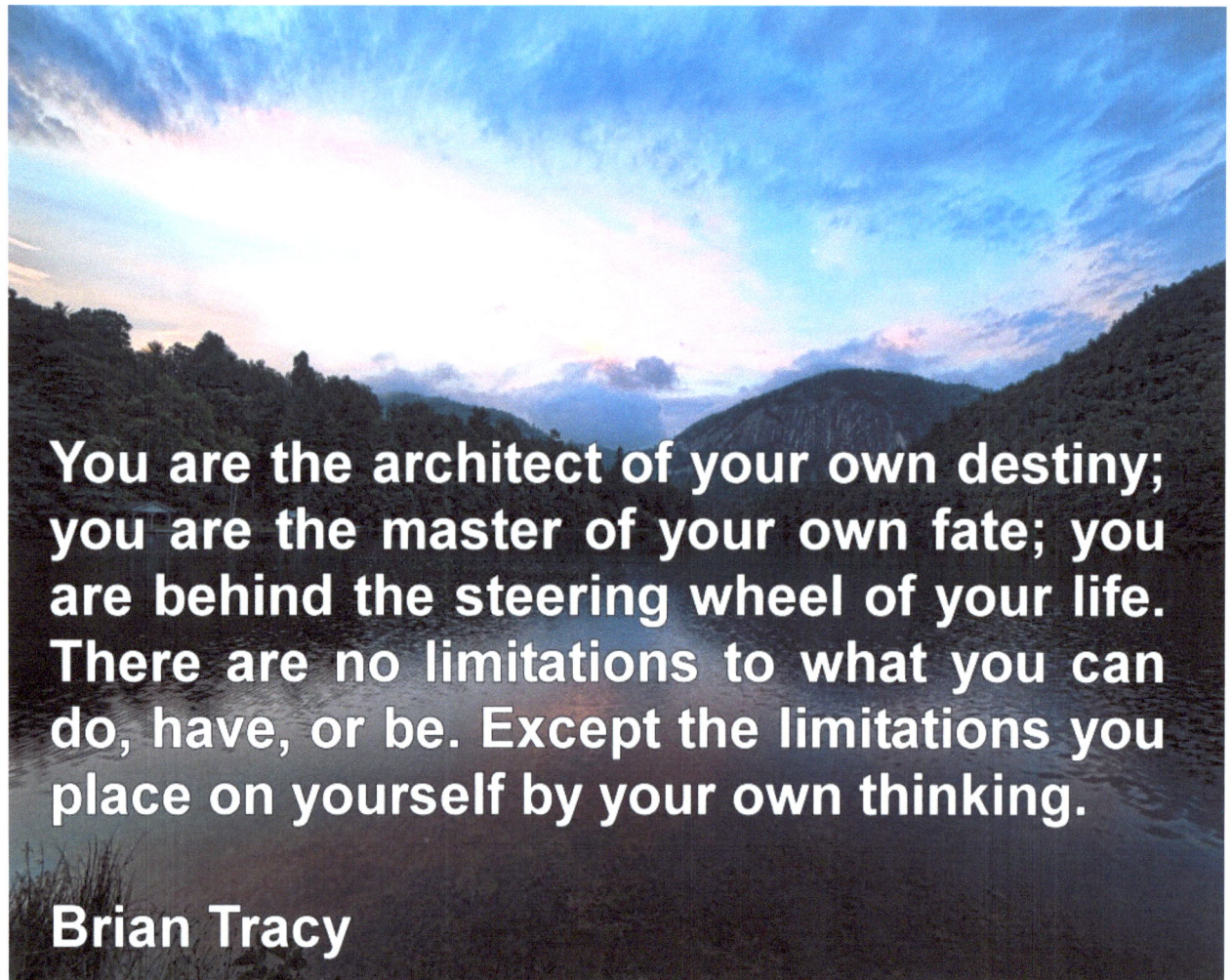

You are the architect of your own destiny; you are the master of your own fate; you are behind the steering wheel of your life. There are no limitations to what you can do, have, or be. Except the limitations you place on yourself by your own thinking.

Brian Tracy

Perception & Physiology

All of our senses are a pathway into our inner pharmacy where tonic thoughts produce tonic chemicals, and toxic thoughts produce toxic chemicals. Stress and negative emotions help produce cortisol, norepinephrine and epinephrine. Relaxation and serenity help to produce dopamine, oxytocin, serotonin and endorphins.

The Stress Response

1 Receptors sense stress stimuli and send chemical signals to the hypothalamus, which releases ACTH to the adrenal glands.

2 The adrenal glands respond with the secretion of cortisol, adrenaline, and noradrenaline to be released into the bloodstream.

3 Immediate physiological changes are induced, including acceleration of heart and lung activity, elevated blood pressure, inhibition of digestive activity, tunnel vision, and sweating.

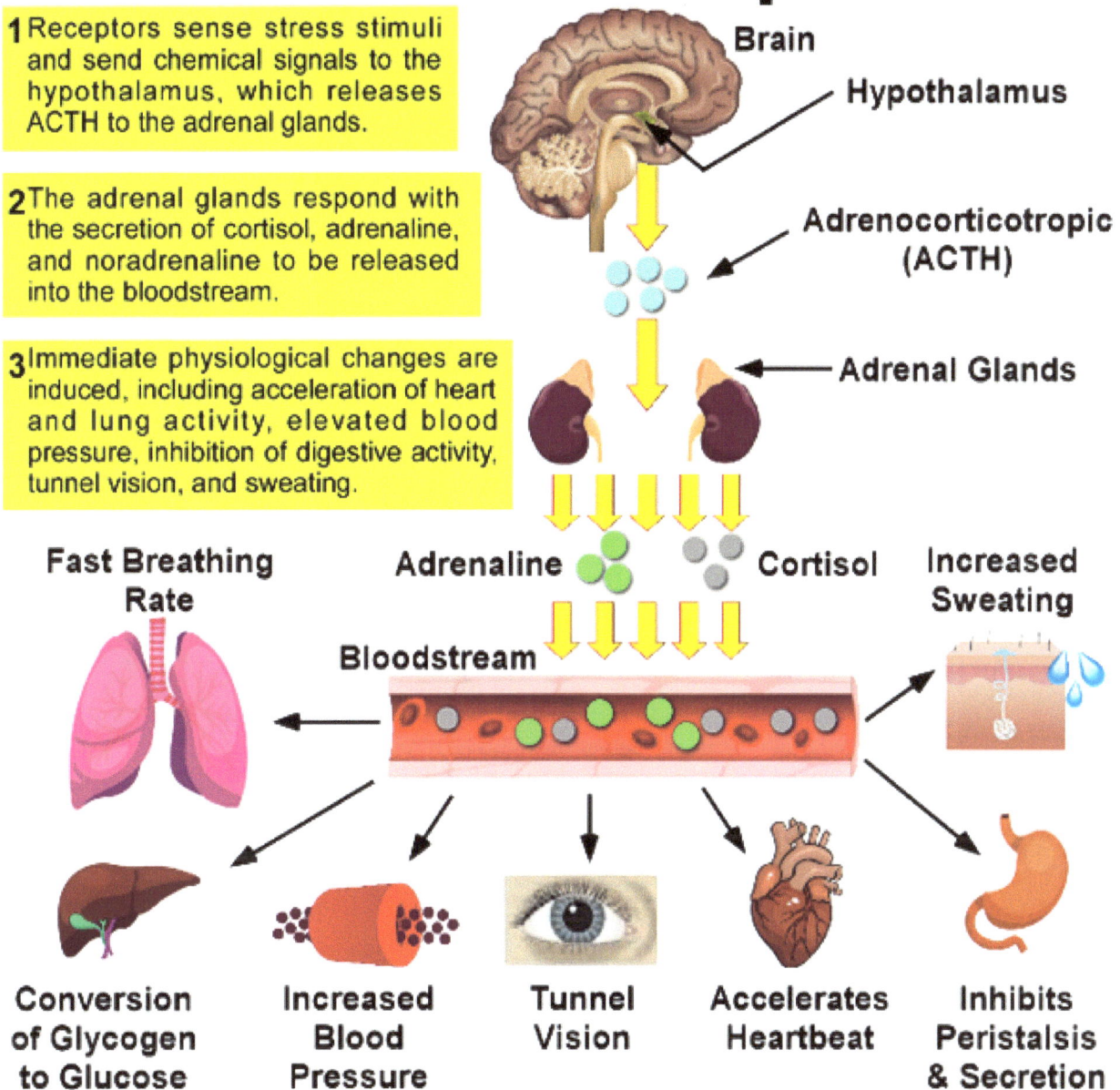

Brain

Hypothalamus

Adrenocorticotropic (ACTH)

Adrenal Glands

Fast Breathing Rate

Adrenaline   Cortisol

Increased Sweating

Bloodstream

Conversion of Glycogen to Glucose

Increased Blood Pressure

Tunnel Vision

Accelerates Heartbeat

Inhibits Peristalsis & Secretion

www.MindandBodyExercises.com

We truly are the architect of our own healing and destiny, where our perspectives and beliefs can shift our own biology and physiology.

Our consciousness is an interpretation of the information that our senses obtain from our immediate internal and external environment.

Our cells adjust their biology from the chemical messengers produced within our body and circulated throughout our blood chemistry.

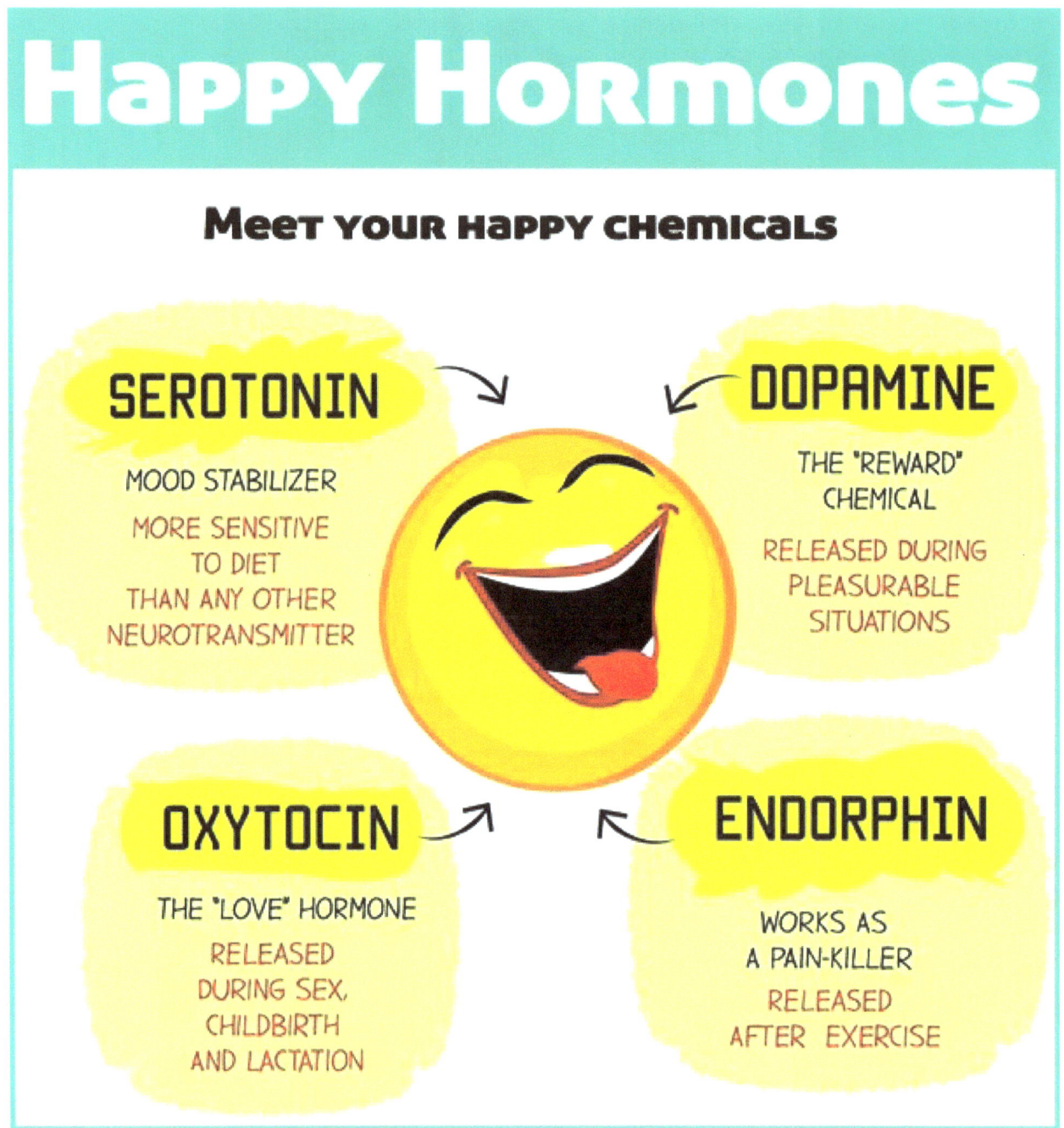

HAPPY HORMONES

MEET YOUR HAPPY CHEMICALS

SEROTONIN
MOOD STABILIZER

MORE SENSITIVE
TO DIET
THAN ANY OTHER
NEUROTRANSMITTER

DOPAMINE
THE "REWARD"
CHEMICAL

RELEASED DURING
PLEASURABLE
SITUATIONS

OXYTOCIN
THE "LOVE" HORMONE

RELEASED
DURING SEX,
CHILDBIRTH
AND LACTATION

ENDORPHIN
WORKS AS
A PAIN-KILLER

RELEASED
AFTER EXERCISE

https://www.kindervelt.org/2020/12/01/happiness-hormone-hacks/

Most people actually have the ability to change the perception of their own environment, thereby adjusting the functions of the cells.

We need not be the victims of our heredity as we change our perception, change our environment and thereby control our genetic activity. We can become the master of our genetic activities.

Our health can be viewed as something that we can regulate through the choices we make in our lives.

What we think, what we feel, what we believe and the emotions we choose to respond with, all affect immunoglobulin A (IGA) in the blood. IGA is the primary defense against bacteria and viruses. circulated in our blood chemistry and affecting relative organ functions.

The moment you change your perception, is the moment you rewrite the chemistry of your body.

— Dr. Bruce Lipton

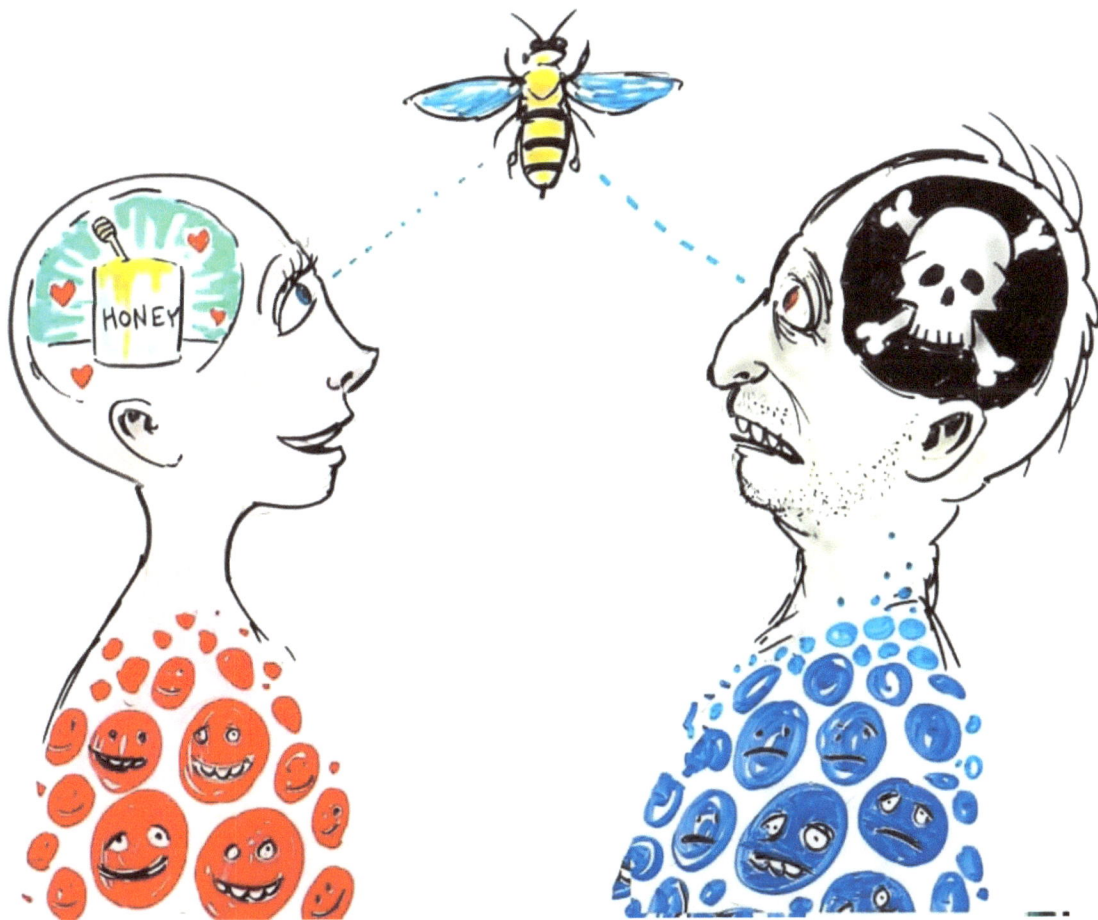

American society has been indoctrinated to believe that Western, conventional or allopathic medical doctors know best for everyone's health and well-being, and the patient should not question this. Pharmaceuticals, surgery and convenience are major components to their healthcare.

Many people have little knowledge of what naturopathy, chiropractic, osteopathy, homeopathy, Ayurveda, Traditional Chinese medicine and others being legitimate healthcare modalities. Western doctors often will not even acknowledge other modalities beyond being placebos, let alone recommend them for a patient's specific individual needs. Ironically, the US allopathic healthcare system also relies substantially on the patient's potential belief in medicine improving their ailment. Factors such as trust in the doctor prescribing the medication, specific details regarding the medicine, like its brand, color, price, name, and place of origin can all affect this perception that medical pharmaceuticals can fix all or many ailments. If placebos can be accepted as a major part of the healing process, more people will be able to take control and accountability of their own well-being. Maybe it truly is "all in our heads".

Hope & Gratitude
People can resist the unfounded fears in their lives. Our bodies know how to be healthy, but our fear affects our body's ability to heal itself.
Our lives are as beautiful or terrible as we choose to perceive them. We have as much or as little opportunity as we choose to pursue.
We can choose to see what an amazing gift it is to be alive. We can choose to focus on love in our lives, of our family and other loved ones. We can choose to be grateful for what we have, and often for what we don't have.
The human body is brilliantly designed to perform seemingly miraculous events of self-regulation and self-healing.
Regardless of how severe or long someone has been ill, there is a hope that they are capable of some level of healing. Many with much less hope or resources, have achieved much more than those with deep pockets, power and celebrity.

We Are Not Our Thoughts
The mind is composed of two independent entities, being the conscious and the subconscious minds.

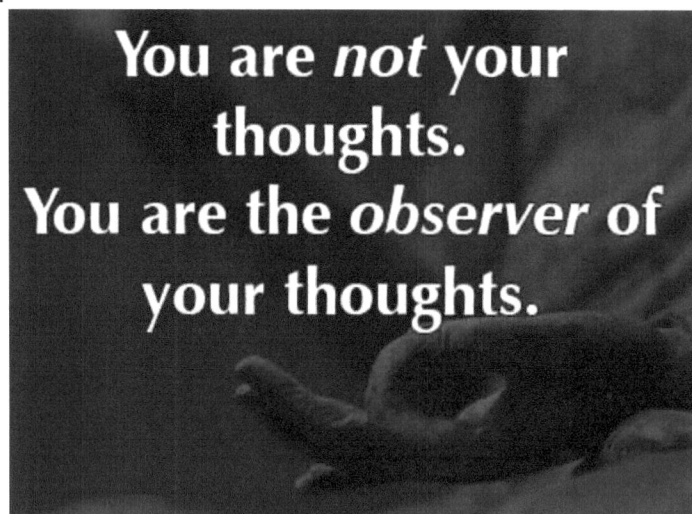

You are *not* your thoughts.
You are the *observer* of your thoughts.

52

The subconscious mind is the default autopilot program, which is where we operate most often throughout our waking hours. This is where we execute mundane tasks, seemingly without much thought or effort. The subconscious mind comes primarily from absorbing other people's behavior and actions.

The conscious mind is the engaged, thinking and creative mind. It is in this state of mind that we can become aware as the observer of our thoughts.

Understand how our mind works, in that it is actually our own consciousness that directs our thoughts and emotions. Once we realize this, we are empowered to become the director of our actions with unlimited potential.

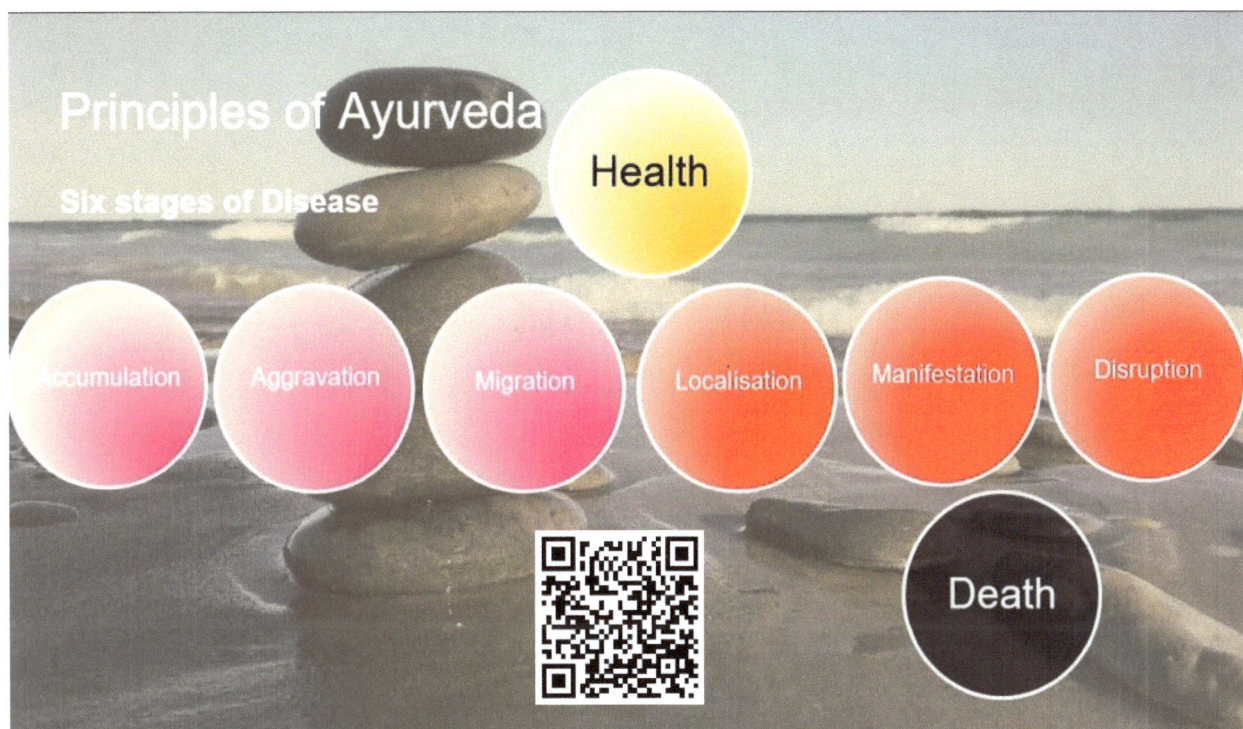

https://www.youtube.com/watch?v=wRx4sINzKT8

Healthcare modalities of Ayurveda and Traditional Chinese Medicine recognize disease as occurring in patterns, cycles or stages. The idea that an individual just becomes ill one day, is hard to acknowledge when obvious patterns in lifestyle choices affect overall health and well-being over the course of a lifetime.

6 Stages of Disease
Six stages of how disease comes into being:
1 – accumulation
2 – aggravation
3 – spread
4 – localization
5 – manifestation

6 – diversified
These stages have everything to do with the individual's own accountability of their health and lifestyle choices and not so much about what others are doing or not doing.
.

The 6 Stages of Fever Related Diseases

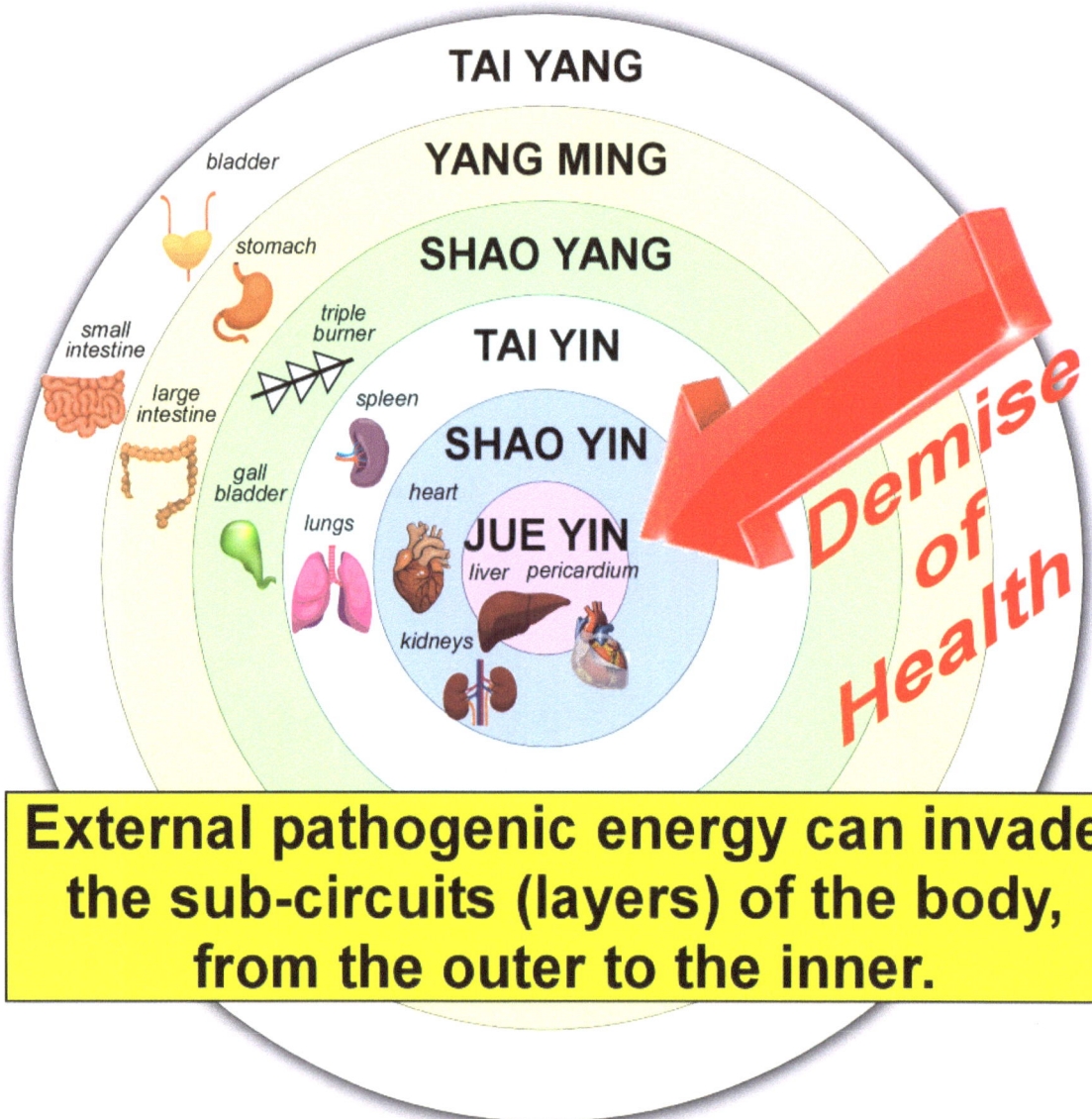

www.MindAndBodyExercises.com © Copyright 2021 - CAD Graphics, Inc.

TCM view of stages of disease

Focus

The world around us is vastly shaped by what we pay attention to at any given moment. Research shows that most people can only hold their attention for about 90 minutes at a time, depending upon their activity or subject. A huge component of focus is motivation. When properly motivated the human mind, body and spirit are quite capable of accomplishing what might have been perceived as improbable or impossible.

People often demonstrate amazing levels of focus when performing skilled work or tasks while using their hands. A theory for this is that such tasks provide a framework of values. It is here where the mind engages the body. Heal the body by using the mind. Heal the mind by engaging the body. This has worked for thousands of years, but in recent years this concept has lost popularity to modern pharmaceuticals to improve focus.

The mind directs the body, while the body protects the mind. Practices such as yoga, tai chi and qigong all have proven the test of time for their healing properties of the mind, body and spirit. I have personally healed many physical injuries to my spine, shoulders, and knees from these methods. I have treated my own ailments of headaches, allergies and various other aches and pains. Additionally, I have addressed and managed other issues of anxiety, grief, and anger through my diligent practices. I have shared these techniques with hundreds and possibly thousands of others, over my years whether through in-person instruction, lectures, publications, or online video classes.

If we can get ourselves all worked up and stressed by watching disturbing news shows or engaging in other negative issues and activities, we can conversely put ourselves in a state of peace, joy or contentment through our thoughts and actions. We are our own architect of our life, our health, our happiness, our destiny.

Choices – we almost always have choices. However, we usually don't like the options.

– junk & fast food vs. healthy unprocessed foods
– elevators vs. stairs
– responsible alcohol consumption vs. drinking to become drunk
– smoking tobacco vs. never even starting
– drive vs. walk
– sit vs. stand
– lounge vs. exercise or activity
– smartphone vs. face-to-face interactions
– watching news or other disturbing info vs. turning it off
– becoming aggravated over things which we have no control vs. controlling what we actually can affect

Self-discipline begins with the mastery of your thoughts. If you don't control what you think, you can't control what you do.

Things We Can Manage

Food & Diet

Exercise

Relationships

Stress Management

Sleep

Most say these are the most important facets in their lives.

Being committed to doing the work and making them a priority is a different discussion.

www.MindAndBodyExercises.com

57

We know these issues to be true, but many don't have the willpower (in the moment) or self-discipline (structured and consistent). Some people innately have self-discipline, while others need to learn and cultivate it. Control the body with the mind. Manage the mind by disciplining the body through physical activity. Learn to be more active, eat healthier, sleep better, stress less – these are the key components to maintaining a strong mind, body, immune system, and outlook on life.

CDC's National Center for Chronic Disease Prevention and Health Promotion (NCCDPHP)

CHRONIC DISEASES IN AMERICA

6 IN 10
Adults in the US
have a **chronic disease**

4 IN 10
Adults in the US
have **two or more**

THE LEADING CAUSES OF DEATH AND DISABILITY
and Leading Drivers of the Nation's **$3.5 Trillion** in Annual Health Care Costs

| HEART DISEASE | CANCER | CHRONIC LUNG DISEASE | STROKE | ALZHEIMER'S DISEASE | DIABETES | CHRONIC KIDNEY DISEASE |

It is almost always easier to maintain something than to fix it once it has broken. The same is true for maintaining health. Why wait for someone to "fix" your health when you have the tools in your own garage? Proper diet, active lifestyle, positive attitude, social interaction - these are the keys to your healthy house.

What Type of House Have We Built?

Our $4 Trillion "Sickcare" System

Order of Appropriate Therapeutic Intervention

Treat the symptoms

8. Surgery

7. Use radiation, chemotherapy

6. Prescribe pharmaceutical substances

5. Prescribe specific modalities for specific conditions and biochemical pathways (botanicals, nutrients, acupuncture, homeopathy, exercise, hydrotherapy, counseling)

4. Correct deficiencies in structural integrity

3. Tonify and nourish weakened systems

2. Stimulate the healing power of nature

1. Reestablish the basis for health:
• Remove obstacles to healing
• Establish a healthy environment
• Address inborn susceptibility

When the healthcare system is based upon a foundation of treating symptoms through diagnosis, pharmaceuticals and often surgery

When the healthcare system is based upon a strong foundation of prevention through diet and lifestyle choices

Treat the root causes

- Little personal responsibility (heal me)

- Pharmaceutical dependence to fix everything

- Root cause never resolved

- Own personal responsibility (heal yourself)

- Diet & herbs balance metabolism

- Root cause addressed

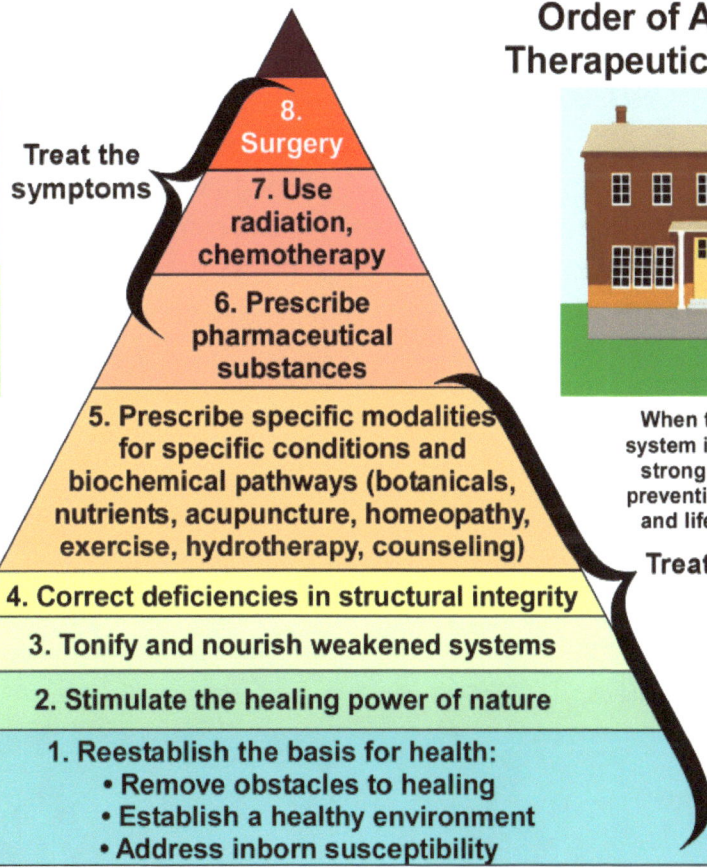

www.MindandBodyExercises.com

© Copyright 2021 - CAD Graphics, Inc.

What You Think Affects Your Health

Many cultures have known this for thousands of years. Western medicine has acknowledged in recent years how stress has an effect on the internal organs and consequently the immune system.

When humans are confronted with trauma or extreme stress, the body adjusts with changes to the blood chemistry to deal with the tasks at hand. When the "fight or flight response" or the parasympathetic nervous system activates, adrenaline and cortisol dump into the blood stream. Prolonged adrenaline & cortisol in the blood is thought to cause deterioration of the internal organs and systems of the human body.

Meditation, tai chi, qigong and yoga are time-proven methods that help regulate thoughts, emotions and the resulting blood chemistry.

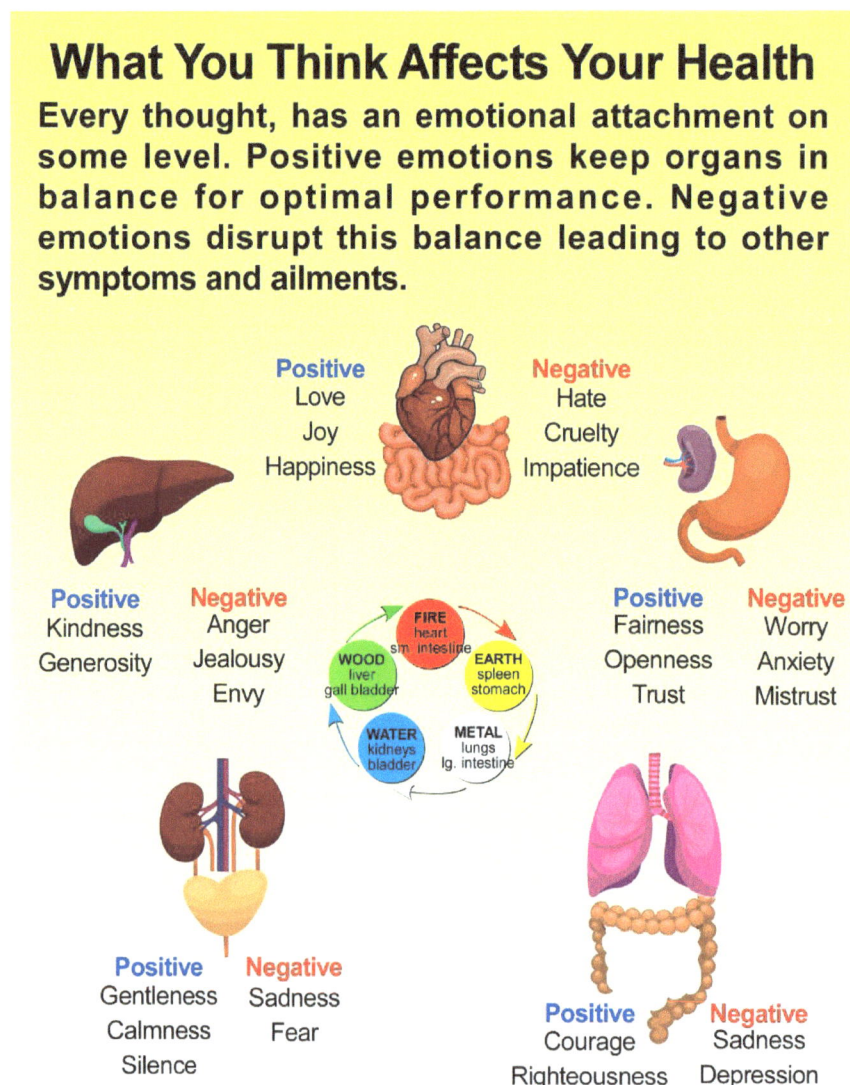

What You Think Affects Your Health

Every thought, has an emotional attachment on some level. Positive emotions keep organs in balance for optimal performance. Negative emotions disrupt this balance leading to other symptoms and ailments.

Positive Love Joy Happiness
Negative Hate Cruelty Impatience

Positive Kindness Generosity
Negative Anger Jealousy Envy

Positive Fairness Openness Trust
Negative Worry Anxiety Mistrust

FIRE heart sm. intestine
WOOD liver gall bladder
EARTH spleen stomach
WATER kidneys bladder
METAL lungs lg. intestine

Positive Gentleness Calmness Silence
Negative Sadness Fear

Positive Courage Righteousness
Negative Sadness Depression

www.MindAndBodyExercises.com

c. Copyright 2020 - CAD Graphics, Inc.

60

Personal Responsibility

We are here…right here where the rubber hits the road.

When the action really begins, is when you begin the job, when you really get serious.
So, the question I have is, how serious are you folks about doing anything? Likes and smiley faces are nice, but really don't make us healthier, fitter, or more connected.

None of us really have "extra" time but rather "make" time for what we prioritize in our lives. True is true, either we walk the talk, or we talk the walk.

Talk is cheap, time is priceless.
If every person in American spent 5 minutes (or more) every day by exercising, more people could better manage their weight and suffer less from related illnesses.

If every person in American spent 5 minutes (or more) every day calming their mind by practicing deep breathing exercises, more people would be less stressed and suffer less from related illnesses.

If every person in American spent every day becoming more conscious of their nutrition habits, more people would be able to maintain their health through the choices they make while eating and drinking and suffer less from related illnesses.

If everyone could assume personal responsibility for their own health, our nation would not have to spend as much time, effort, energy and money trying to keep people healthy.

These concepts seem easy enough, but in reality, most people lack the desire or self-discipline to make the effort and do what it takes to stay healthy, prevent illness or cure their own ailments. Self-discipline is one of five steps known to help achieve better mental and physical wellness.

1) **Respect** – This is where values begin. You must understand and have respect for yourself (self-respect) before you can demonstrate it to others. Taking the steps to take care of your physical and mental well-being affects you first and then those closest to you second.
2) **Discipline** – Developing control of one's own desires, commitments, and ultimately your own actions, leads to self-discipline. Control of physical exercises can lead to management of thought and emotion.
3) **Self-Esteem** – As you review your achievements of respect and discipline, your sense of worth is elevated and appreciated.
4) **Confidence** – Understanding and accepting your weak areas as well as your stronger aspects removes insecurity. When you feel that you are physically well and mentally sharp, confidence can fill your personality. You can accomplish whatever goal you set out to achieve.
5) **Determination to Achieve Goals** – The positive sum of the previous aspects leads to one's determination. Good judgment and focused effort toward positive goals result in true personal success.

Qigong, Tai Chi and Yoga all are methods to achieve these traits.

It doesn't matter so much that you do these exercises, as much as it matters that you do some type of exercise. Walk, jog, swim or whatever – just get going and do something. 5 minutes here and there can quickly turn into 15 or 30 minutes at one time or over the course of a day. Once you are moving or mentally engaged, it is much easier to stay motivated and try a few more exercises for a few more minutes.

A Balanced Life - One Perspective

A Balanced Life - One Perspective

Mind **Body**

Spirit

Intent
Intellect
Inner dialogue
Positive attitude
Personal boundaries
Emotion management

Physical health
Proper nutrition
Adequate sleep
Personal hygiene
Stress management
Exercise and movement
Responsible medical care
Preservation of resources

Self-awareness
Values & morals
Sense of purpose
Seeing yourself, as others see you
Faith in something bigger than yourself

Often, I hear or read about the discussion of the mind, body & spirit connection, or achieving the harmony of all three. I have been studying, practicing and pursuing this harmony for over 40 years. I have found that this balance doesn't just come about; it takes time, effort, resources, sacrifice or some combination of these factors.

Mind, body & spiritual well-being don't recognize the gym, the yoga studio, the spa. Nor does the designer workout clothes and gear. It is not about the stuff, the equipment, the place.

It is, however, about the individual committing themselves to be the best version of themselves. The other items are just tools to help with the journey along the way.

A Method to Pursue Mind, Body & Spirit Harmony - The 8-Step Path

A long-understood method of achieving harmony between one's mind, body and spirit, is this 8-Step Path. It has its origin in the ancient Chinese philosophy of Daoism but is highly relative to modern culture. The figure "8" is important to understand that as the infinity circle, there is no beginning nor end to entering into this process. It is a journey of self-awareness that can be entered into at any point throughout one's lifetime. Life is a challenge and so is staying on this path of self-improvement. The reward is at the end of one's journey, knowing that they have pursued a meaningful life with direction and purpose.

Spirituality and religion are often lumped together but have rather distinctly different meanings. So, let's look at spiritually more as a level of self-awareness, purpose and life direction and not necessarily a membership to any particular religion or belief system.

The graphics below shows how the 8 are all interconnected. Below are the brief descriptions of each of the 8 steps. This is by no means the only method to find this harmony of mind, body and spirit. It is a time-proven method that I have learned and have tried to cultivate for many years.

Eight Keys of Wisdom

Reflection

Make correct choices

Overcome your delusion

Turn on your light

Attain honor

Change your reality

Become a vessel of wisdom

Draw from nature's energies

The 8-Step Path to Achieve the Best Version of You   www.MindAndBodyExercises.com

A long-understood method of achieving harmony between one's mind, body and spirit, is this 8-Step Path. It has its origin in the ancient Chinese philosophy of Daoism but is highly relative to modern culture. The figure "8" is important to understand that as the infinity circle, there is no beginning nor end to entering into this process. It is a journey of self-awareness that can be entered into at any point throughout one's lifetime. Life is a challenge, and so is staying on this path of self-improvement. The reward is at the end of one's journey, knowing that they have pursued a meaningful life with direction and purpose.

1 Learning to Know Your "True Self"
By seeing & understanding your nature, self-reflection opens the door to the other steps of this process.

2 Making Correct Daily Choices
True
Right ← Correct
Awareness of an inner "Moral Compass" to balance decisions by understanding true, right & correct.

3 Overcome Delusion of Your Thoughts & Ideas
You are not your thoughts. As consciousness you control your thoughts. Try not to be swayed by the mundane & trivial. Be solid like the root & not flippant like the leaves.

4 Cultivate Good Seeds to Pass On
Realize that you have a higher purpose beyond gaining material wealth and status. Be the light at the end of the tunnel.

5 Attain Honor
Live by principle - stand firm in what you believe, while allowing challenges to flow around you. Stand like a mountain, flow like a river.

6 Change Your Reality
Understand that you are in control of your life and the choices you make determine your success or failure within your reality.

7 Become a Living Vessel of Wisdom
Knowledge alone is not power. The sharing of our knowledge, is when knowledge becomes powerful.

8 Draw on Nature's Power
fire water wind
Qigong Tai Chi Baguazhang
Cultivate a strong mind, body & spirit by connecting to nature's fire, water & wind with sitting, standing & moving exercises.

65

1 Learning to Know Your "True Self"

By seeing & understanding your nature, self-reflection opens the door to the other steps of this process.

2 Making Correct Daily Choices

True

Right ← **Correct**

Awareness of an inner "Moral Compass" to balance decisions by understanding true, right & correct.

3 Overcome Delusion of Your Thoughts & Ideas

You are not your thoughts. As consciousness you control your thoughts. Try not to be swayed by the mundane & trivial. Be solid like the root & not flippant like the leaves.

4 Cultivate Good Seeds to Pass On

Realize that you have a higher purpose beyond gaining material wealth and status. Be the light at the end of the tunnel.

5 Attain Honor

Live by principle - stand firm in
what you believe, while allowing
challenges to flow around you.
Stand like a mountain,
flow like a river.

6 Change Your Reality

Understand that you are in control
of your life and the choices you
make determine your success
or failure within your reality.

7 Become a Living Vessel of Wisdom

Knowledge alone is not power.
The sharing of our knowledge,
is when knowledge becomes
powerful.

8 Draw on Nature's Power

fire   water   wind

Qigong   **Tai Chi**   **Baguazhang**

Cultivate a strong mind, body &
spirit by connecting to nature's
fire, water & wind with sitting,
standing & moving exercises.

Qigong, tai chi, BaguaZhang, and yoga are not the only methods that can be used within this formula but have proven the test of time as methods to cultivate harmony of the mind, body and spirit. These exercise practices offer a wide spectrum of physical wellness benefits, stress relief as well as a means of self-awareness. Not all teachers nor students practice these for the same goals.

_____

Discipline the mind to discipline the body

Anything of value is always going to require some amount of sacrifice of time, effort and resources.

Self-discipline begins with the mastery of your thoughts. If you don't control what you think, you can't control what you do.

For most people, it is very difficult to train or discipline their mind and consequently, their body. People often say or do things they regret only to realize later that they lacked the self-control and self-awareness to make good decisions to begin with.

By gaining control of the physical anatomy, a relationship with the physical body is developed. When aligning the limbs and joints to stretch and strengthen them, while also maintaining deep and deliberate breathing rhythms, an individual can cultivate a more harmonious link between the mind, body and spirit (self-awareness). Practice exercises that truly engage the mind and body, (very much like yoga) to improve health & wellness. The mind directs the body, while the body protects the mind.

Increase the Capacity of Your Nervous System

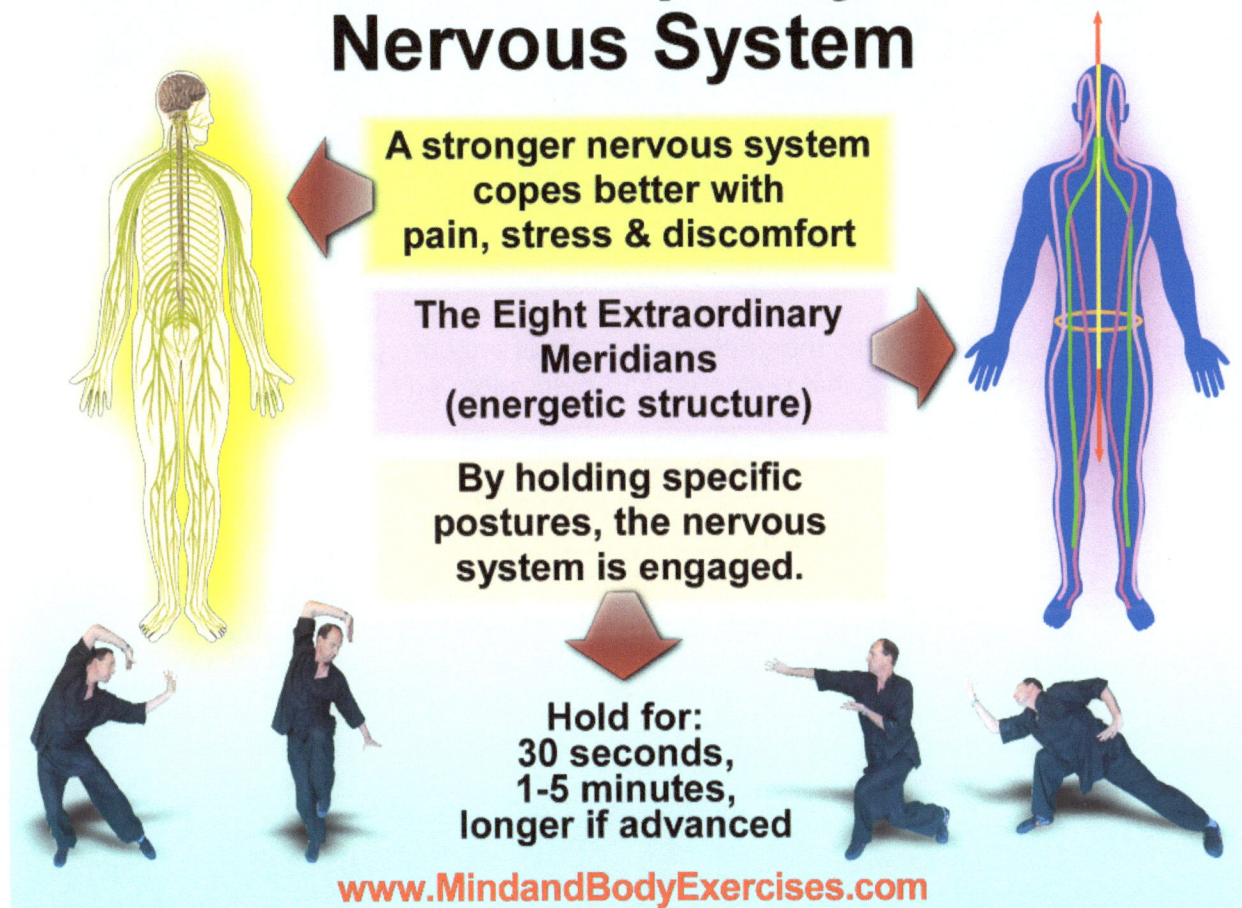

A stronger nervous system copes better with pain, stress & discomfort

The Eight Extraordinary Meridians (energetic structure)

By holding specific postures, the nervous system is engaged.

Hold for:
30 seconds,
1-5 minutes,
longer if advanced

www.MindandBodyExercises.com

Ship Pal Gye, Taoist yoga or the "Filling the 8 Vessels" are methods to increase the capacity of your nervous system. By holding the body in specific alignments, the nervous system is strengthened to endure more pain, stress and discomfort. Think of tempering steel in fire to strengthen the metal. Building self-discipline of the mind and body simultaneously!

When engaging the muscles, tendons, bones and fascia, the 12 regular energy meridians are engaged plus the 8 extraordinary meridians are opened and filled as reservoirs to adjust the ebb and flow of energy throughout the body and thereby strengthening the immune system among other bodily functions.

Exercise methods like these have been known for centuries but are considered new or "alternative" to modern western culture.

Watch the video at the link below to get a sample of what this type of instruction entails. Often times people will ask me, "where did you learn this?" Well...almost 40 years ago I began studying Korean kung fu, then Traditional Chinese Medicine, medical qigong, fitness, wellness and anatomy. It didn't happen overnight or from a weekend seminar. It took me

71

decades of learning, studying and teaching from and with high level masters and teachers. And I'm not done learning yet, are you?

https://youtu.be/dD3w7_Hgp8I

Energy Flow Within the Body

Circulation is also increased as the gentle squishing of the core provides a "tourniquet effect" of the blood flow being somewhat restricted and then released to flush through the veins and arteries.

The Tourniquet Effect

These graphics illustrates the twisting of the body and its various systems. The tourniquet effect restricts and then releases the blood and thus, energy flow to a specific organ, muscle or joint. Veins, arteries and organs are cleaned out, flushed with fresh blood and oxygen. The same events affect the joints, by flushing through breaking down scar tissue and improving the quality of synovial fluids. This can help prevent and eliminate tendinitis, arthritis and many other circulation issues.

Regulated Breathing

Typical daily breathing is usually between 12-18 breaths per minute (BPM). When breaths slow to below 10 BPM, the parasympathetic nervous system is activated. Breathing in timed rhythm or to music at a 4/4 measure (4 seconds to inhale; 4 seconds to exhale) drops the BPM to about 7.5 BPM, thereby engaging the body into the restful benefits of a good night's sleep, while awake.

72

Grow Older, but Also Grow Wiser

We all grow older, but do we ever really grow up? Growing up usually refers to being more responsible, more independent, more aware, more giving of oneself.

However, it usually takes a better part of a lifetime to realize what is most important in our lives. Our family and our health, right? How cliché. We say it because it sounds wise and moral. But really, what we as humans seem to value the most is our home, cars, money, and other material possessions. Our ego tops the list of our priorities as we like to think that what we offer more than we receive in our daily existence within the universe.

Often, we look to point out how others should be better. Another perspective would be to make ourselves better. Be the best version of ourselves that we can be. Set an example because this action alone can be contagious in a positive way.

Wisdom is a recipe of knowledge and experience obtained over time (age) allowing one to differentiate when the correct timing is to react or not to react. When to do, when not to do. Coming up to a stop sign, you really don't care to stop your vehicle (your true feeling) but you do because it is the right action (the law) to stop. If a blaring fire engine were to suddenly appear in your rear-view mirror, you might choose to move through the intersection and to a space clear of the oncoming 370,000 pounds of moving metal and water (correct action for this situation).

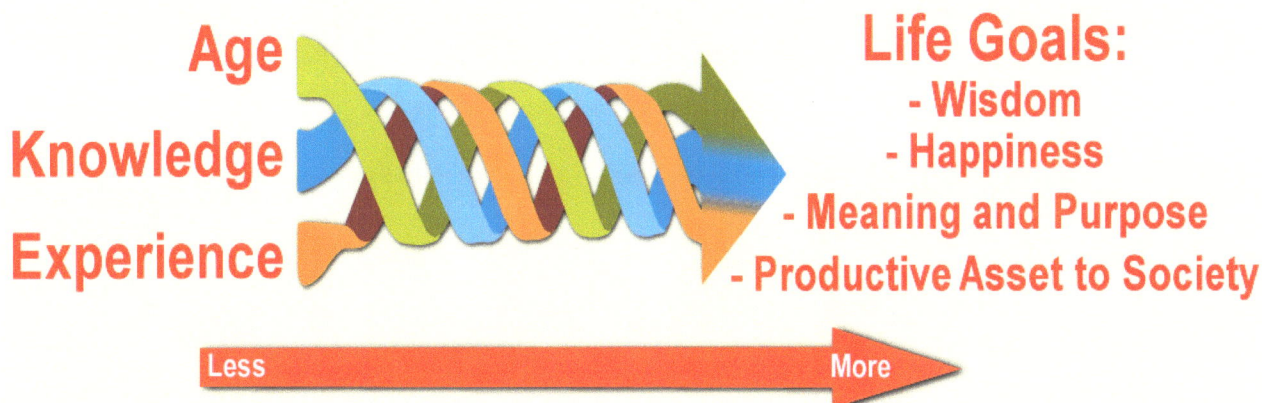

Grow Older, But Also Grow Wiser

Age
Knowledge
Experience

Life Goals:
- Wisdom
- Happiness
- Meaning and Purpose
- Productive Asset to Society

Less   More

www.MindAndBodyExercises.com   (C) Copyright 2020 - CAD Graphics, Inc.

Many chronic health issues can be managed or eliminated with appropriate knowledge of how the human body works. Ailments such as joint or muscular pain are often due to injury or postural issues. Proper knowledge of exercise and physical movement can usually help. Issues such as stress, headaches, high blood pressure, obesity and many others can be improved through the appropriate methods for each individual's personal situation.

Additionally, many emotional and mental issues can be improved or managed through skillful practices that engage the individual's mind and body simultaneously. Examples of mind and body engaging methods would be tai chi, yoga, Pilates, and meditation. Other methods might include playing a musical instrument, painting or engaging in nature.

Referred Pain In One Area Can Be Felt Elsewhere

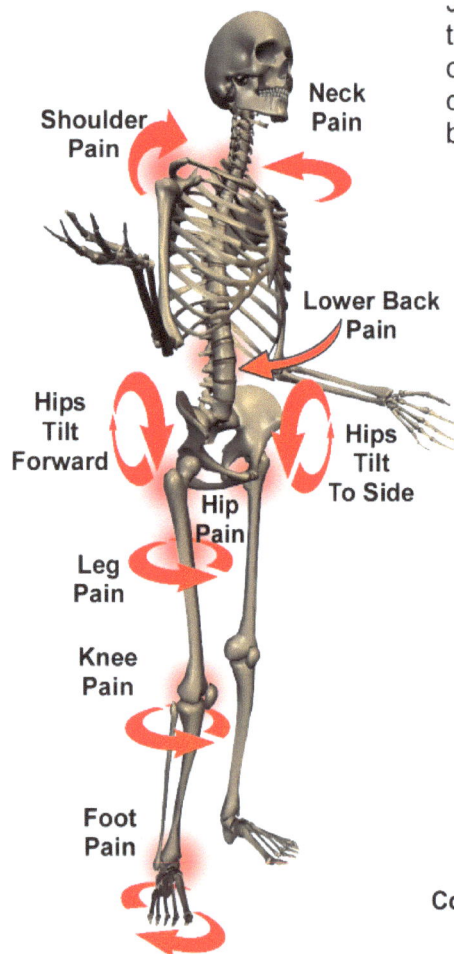

Just like the tensegrity model, tension on one area of the body can affect tension on all components throughout the human body.

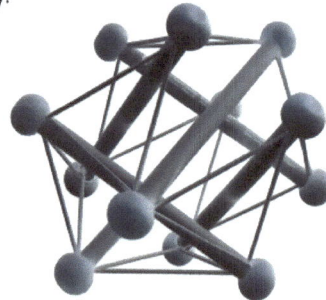

Neck Pain

Shoulder Pain

Lower Back Pain

Hips Tilt Forward

Hips Tilt To Side

Hip Pain

Leg Pain

Knee Pain

Foot Pain

A lateral rotation of the hips can lead also to an anterior tilt called Lordosis.

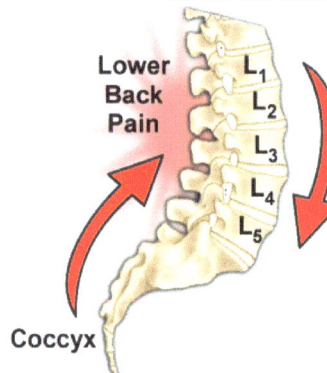

Lower Back Pain

L_1 L_2 L_3 L_4 L_5

Coccyx

www.MindAndBodyExercises.com

(c) Copyright 2021 - CAD Graphics, Inc.

Methods to Improve Imbalances

Course of Action:

- consult with your physician or chiropractor
- have your posture checked
- stretch regularly
- perform non-specific symmetrical exercises
- inspect footwear for uneven wear patterns
- evaluate poor posture habits and adjust
- review career choices if necessary

There are many individual exercises and techniques, that can stretch and release tension of the fascia trains throughout the human body. Tai Chi, Qigong, Yoga and Pilates are methods of stretching and strengthening the fascia as preventative or post-injury low impact exercises.

www.MindAndBodyExercises.com

© Copyright 2021 - CAD Graphics, Inc.

Humans Have Become Disconnected From Nature

Humans have gradually been losing their connection with nature. It did not happen overnight, but maybe most apparently over the last century. Many now believe that synthetic is better than organic as a rule, rather than the exception. The most scientifically, industrialized, modernized aware specie on the earth – while being the unhealthiest specie as a whole. And here we are.

My understanding is that if we do not learn to exist in harmony within nature, we will eventually be consumed by nature. As humans, we are part of nature so we cannot separate ourselves from nature and really the universe, without suffering some type of consequence. Cause and effect, yin and yang – it is all the same; everything is interconnected on many levels.

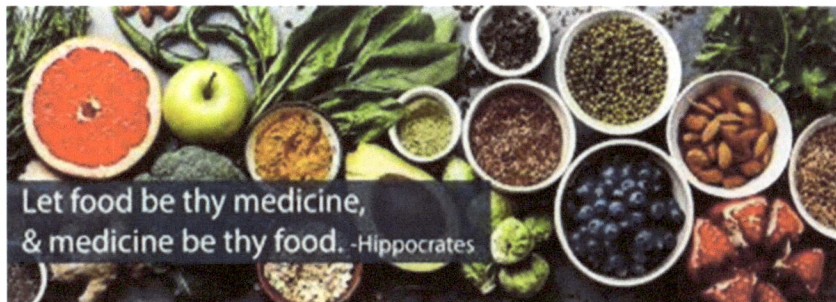

Let food be thy medicine, & medicine be thy food. -Hippocrates

I feel there has been a big disconnect over the last 100 years in that with the advancement of Western allopathic medicine and its many benefits, we have been taught that many of nature's cures and remedies are quackery or limited in their benefits to our modern society. How far have we been distracted to believe that pills and pharmaceuticals are the only way to treat illness and disease? Many people can, and do manage stress, depression, anxiety, high blood pressure, headaches, allergies and maybe an endless list of other ailments that can be improved through proper diet of chemical-free foods and herbs, consistent exercise (natural movement) and management of thoughts and emotions (an understanding of where humans fit into nature). Nature is indeed medicine, as food tends to be either medicine or poison, especially becoming more evident as we age.

Many parents have helped to encourage generations of children who prefer sitting in front of the TV, computer or smartphone screens in place of physical outdoor nature related activities. Children playing and exploring in nature, have become mostly a thing of the past as these same children have grown to be adults with no connection to the nature and wildlife existing in their own backyards.

Look at some of the bigger U.S. cities that have been covered in concrete and metal. Much of the grass and trees have been removed to make way for buildings and development. Some cities like Chicago, New York City, Boston, Miami and others have relatively small parks to help those in need of some "green space" to have an access point to some plant life. Some buildings have gardens or plant life on their roofs, but really these are not grounded to the actual earth below. Other cities like Atlanta and Dallas have made great strides in increasing their public parks and green spaces.

Another example, however more controversial, is the overall health of the human race today. Food producers have been able to provide more food for more people although there are still many starving nations. With advancements in chemicals used to make food look better, last longer and seem tastier, we now ingest these same chemicals which have been proven to cause many other health issues. Americans often have access to many food options but seem to favor cheaper processed foods over the more expensive organic or supposedly chemical-free foods. Then when people develop illnesses from the poor-quality food, they turn to more chemicals through pharmaceuticals to fix the ailments caused by the chemicals in the food. More chemicals in the human body make the individual more dependent upon modern chemistry rather than using nature's gift of fruits, vegetables and herbs that have been known to improve many ailments.

I feel more connected to nature because I choose to be and can make plans and adjustments to be in nature. However, I know that I can be more in nature and that is where the struggle can exist for me. For me, nature is not just a place in the woods or in the mountains. Nor is it a place in a movie, book or a picture although these modes can put my thoughts of a place in nature in my mind. So, where I don't always have the trees, streams and wildlife right in front of me, I do carry the awareness without them to realize that I do have my connection to nature (and the universe) regardless of if I am in the forest or in a concrete building. This awareness is what gets me out of the building to begin with. We exist within nature as much as nature exists within us. Yin and yang in all things. I try to connect daily with nature if not through physically being within the woods, mountains or oceans but through my meditation and awareness of nature.

I think that if someone opens up their mind to understand that we are all interconnected with nature, the universe and each other, nature will present itself in ways and experiences that most people would consider to be far outside of what most to believe as "normal". I am also a professional photographer, who has had many occasions where I sat and waited for a particular image to develop in my mind and then sometimes minutes later in reality. I waited for the sky to clear and then present beautiful rainbows. I was at a cemetery once searching for my relative's gravesite, when a sun shower started exactly when I looked down to see the tombstone I was looking for. I was hiking with my wife in Zion, and while we looked for cover on the trail from harsh rain, a boulder came crashing down on the trail where we had been standing moments earlier. I think that if you try to make these types of experiences happen, they probably will not. However, if you can enter into a perspective that all and everything is interconnected on various levels, things will present themselves to us for whatever reason, lesson or thing is to be gained from such events.

Learning Before Earning

Seems like a fairly simple concept, right?

For example, in the US an individual needs to go through the school system at least until 16 years old, before they can start working to earn an income. Then one can possibly move on to trade school, college, the military or other further education to elevate their knowledge base to their next level. ***Or not!*** Some people enter into the work force, take care of family or friends, or move onto other modes of becoming what is considered a successful life. With *age*, *knowledge* and *life* experience, I have found that all roads basically lead to the same goals of:

- Pursuing health and happiness
- Living with meaning and purpose
- Becoming an asset to society
- Acquiring wisdom throughout one's life

Unless someone is independently wealthy and has innate knowledge of how to manage their resources, they need to have some plan to gain the knowledge in order to achieve the above facets of life.

Review the following graphics to see the logical progression of achieving a well-earned life. Learn before earning. Never stop learning; never stop earning. Invest in yourself.

FIRST LEARN
THEN REMOVE L

Graduate From High School

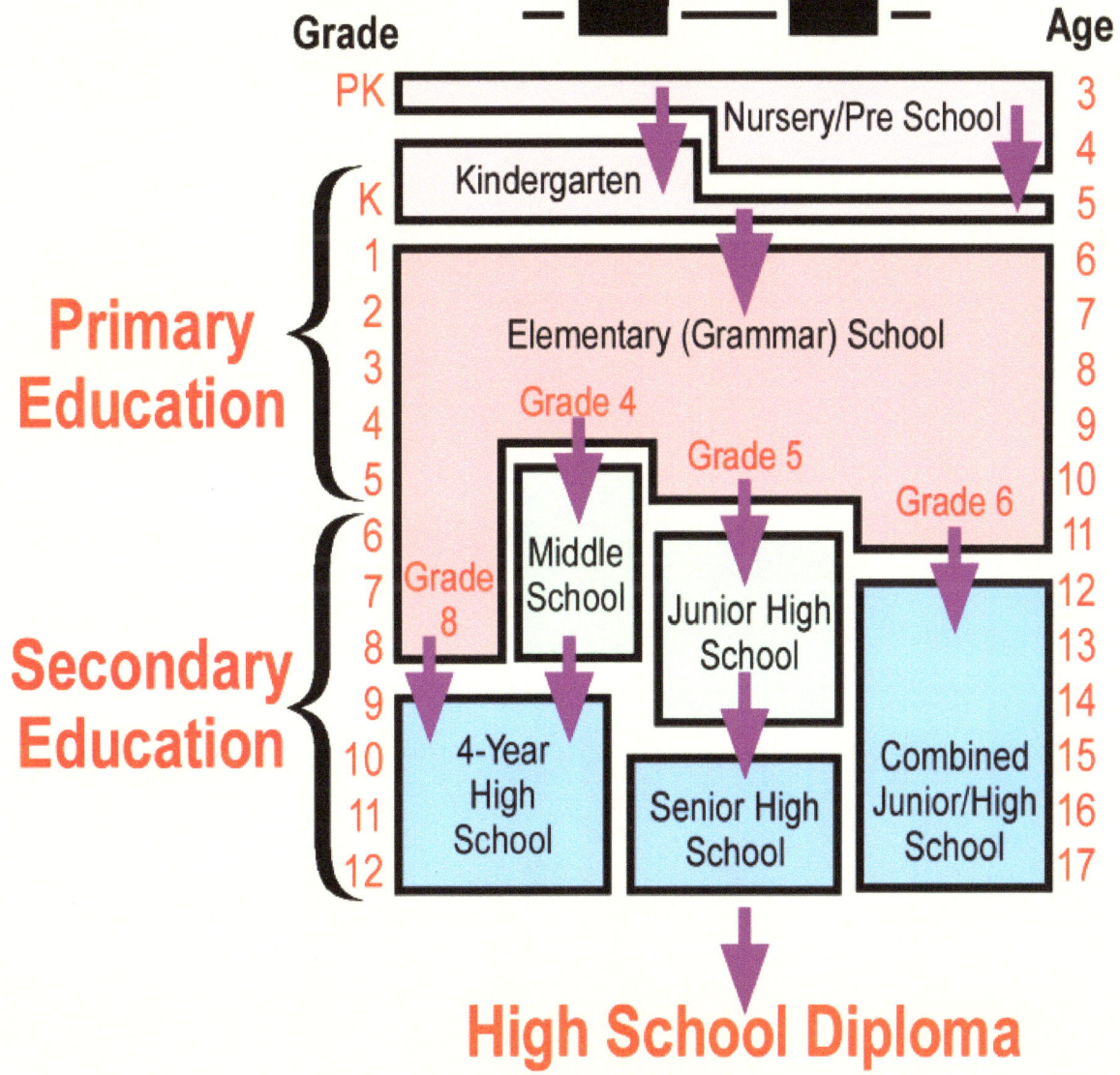

Grade | Age

Grade		Age
PK	Nursery/Pre School	3
		4
K	Kindergarten	5
1		6
2	Elementary (Grammar) School	7
3		8
4		9
5		10

Primary Education

Grade 4

Grade 5

Grade 6

Secondary Education

6		11
7	Middle School	12
8	Junior High School	13
9	Combined Junior/High School	14
10	4-Year High School	15
11	Senior High School	16
12		17

Grade 8

High School Diploma

Further Your Knowledge

Establish A Career

High School Diploma

Years

1	Junior or Community Colleges	Vocation Technical Institutions
2		

Associate's Degree or Certificate

Tertiary Education

Undergraduate Programs — Bachelor's Degree

Master Degree Studies

Professional Schools (medicine, Theology, Law, etc.) — Master's Degree

Doctoral Studies

Ph.D. or Advanced Professional Degree

Postdoctoral Studies & Research

Full-time Parenting or Caretaking

Military Options

Trade School or Apprenticeships

Employment With On-the-job Training

Other Paths

Earn a Living

Life Goals
- Wisdom
- Happiness
- Meaning and Purpose
- Productive Asset to Society

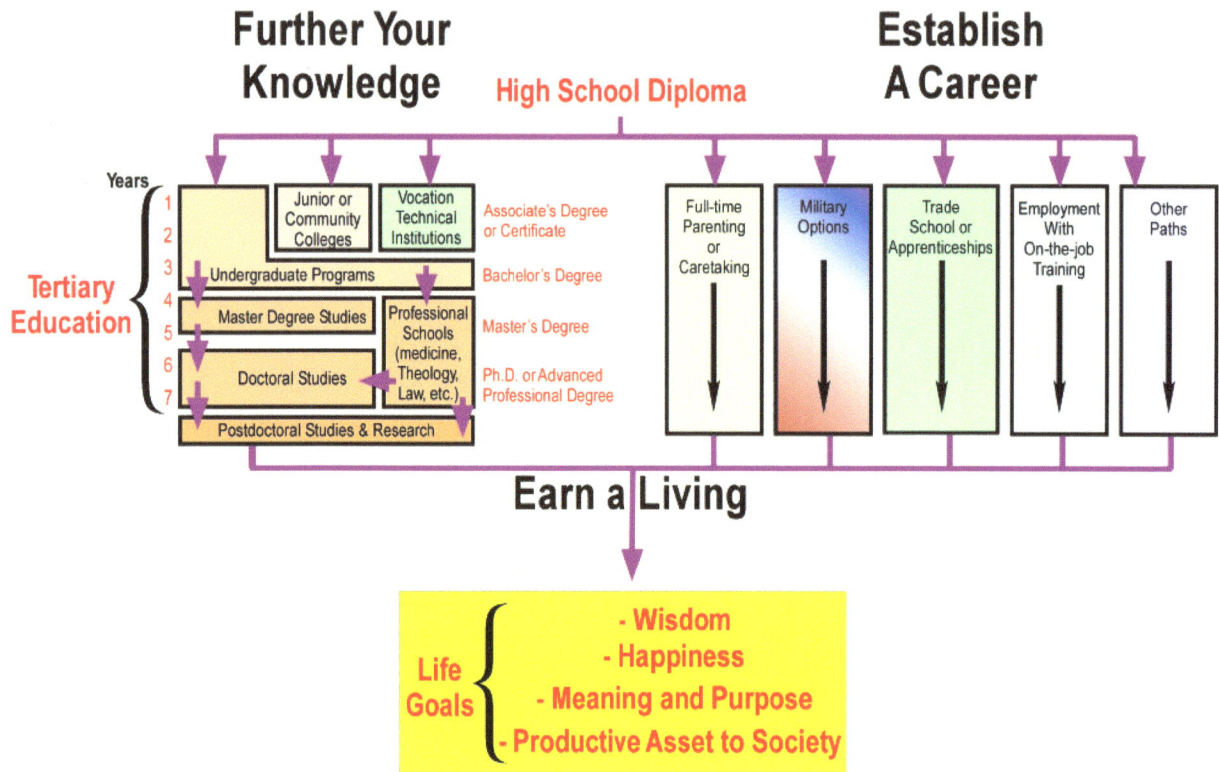

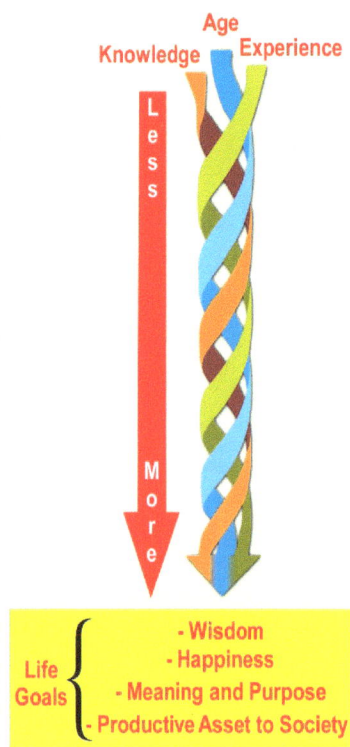

Knowledge   Age   Experience

Less

More

Life Goals
- Wisdom
- Happiness
- Meaning and Purpose
- Productive Asset to Society

82

Typical Education/Life Paths

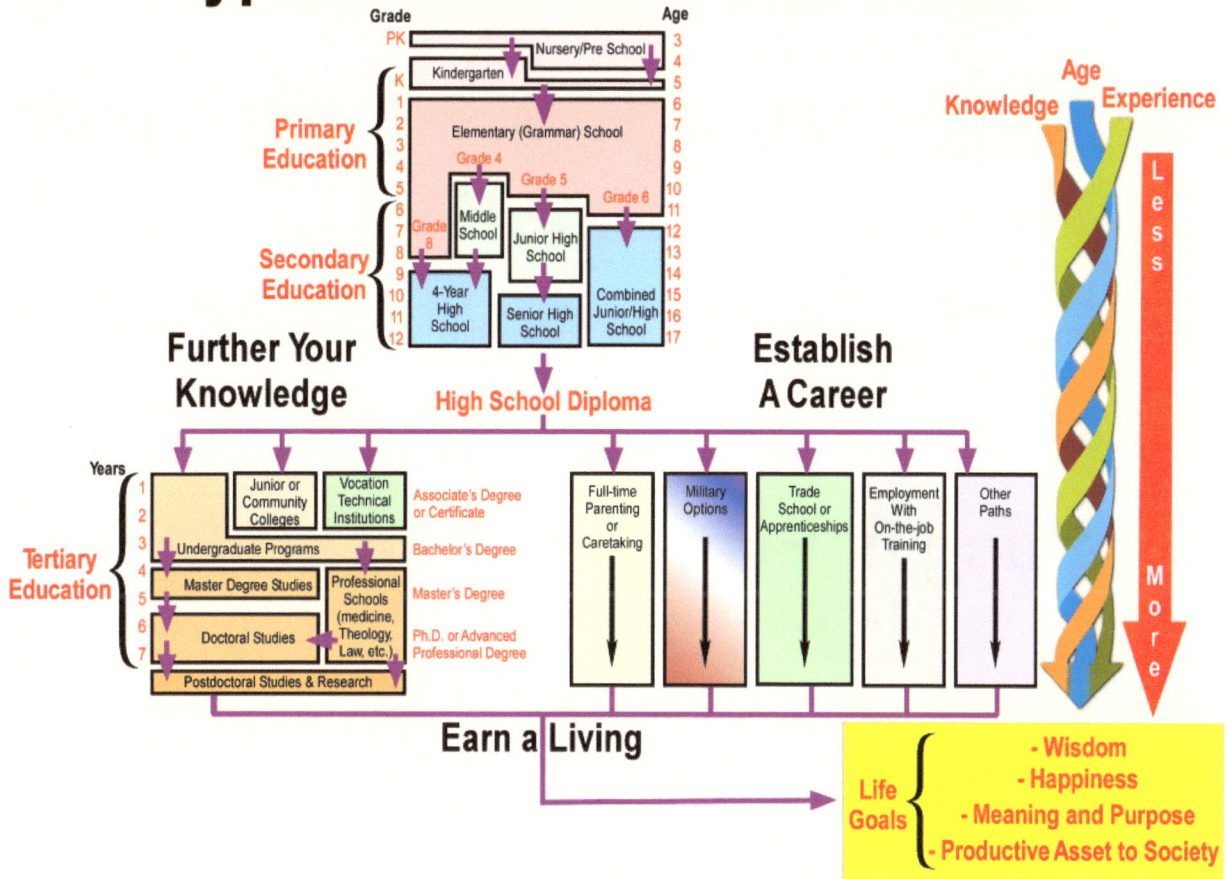

Primary Education

Secondary Education

Further Your Knowledge

Establish A Career

Grade / Age

PK — Nursery/Pre School — 3, 4
Kindergarten — K, 5
Elementary (Grammar) School — 1, 2, 3, 4, 5 — 6, 7, 8, 9, 10
Grade 4, Grade 5, Grade 6
Middle School — Junior High School — Combined Junior/High School
4-Year High School — Senior High School
Grade 8

Knowledge — Age — Experience

Less — More

High School Diploma

Years			
1	Junior or Community Colleges	Vocation Technical Institutions	Associate's Degree or Certificate
2			
3	Undergraduate Programs		Bachelor's Degree
4	Master Degree Studies	Professional Schools (medicine, Theology, Law, etc.)	Master's Degree
5			
6	Doctoral Studies		Ph.D. or Advanced Professional Degree
7			
	Postdoctoral Studies & Research		

Tertiary Education

Full-time Parenting or Caretaking

Military Options

Trade School or Apprenticeships

Employment With On-the-job Training

Other Paths

Earn a Living

Life Goals
- Wisdom
- Happiness
- Meaning and Purpose
- Productive Asset to Society

www.MindAndBodyExercises.com

© Copyright 2020 - CAD Graphics, Inc.

83

Yin and Yang - a very old concept that has been studied for thousands of years by many cultures.

Everything exists in a state of constant change, balance and relevance. What works at one moment, does not a moment later. What appears one way, is seen completely different from another perspective. Without the mind, there is no body. Daytime transforms into nighttime. And so, the cycles continue.

Deep wisdom and lessons can be learned from such a simple law of nature.

Nothing is Ever Just Black & White
The Concept of Yin & Yang

Yin & Yang are relative terms, in relation to content and context. In the concept of Yin & Yang, nothing is permanent nor absolute. Opposites are complementary. Many philosophers and scholars view Yin & Yang as the motive force for the start, change and end of life. Traditional Chinese Medicine (TCM) is based upon the belief that the existence of the universe is due to the result of the interactions between Yin & Yang.

Here is the "dark"

Here is the "Light"

Here is the "dark" that is in the "light"

Here is the "light" that is in the "dark"

Here is Life, with light & dark continuously changing & balancing

© Copyright 2020 - CAD Graphics, Inc.

www.MindAndBodyExercises.com

84

The 5 Element Theory - the 5 Seasons of Life

Sometimes we forget how much our lives are dependent upon the seasons of the year. Not just what jacket to wear or which food is in season, but rather how our mind and body interact with the cycles of nature. For example, should an 8-year-old engage in technical mountain climbing while an 80-year-old attempts to play football? A teenager can eat non-stop where a 50-ish person can get by on much less.

Of course, there are exceptions with various individuals and their level of health and fitness. Do you know where you are at in the seasons of your life and how you can be mindful of what you eat, what type of exercise you engage in, what your thoughts are focused upon? The philosophy behind many of the Far Eastern practices of Qigong, Tai Chi and Traditional Chinese Medicine (TCM) are all about becoming aware of these aspects and how to balance them within your life.

Seasons of Life - 5 Elements

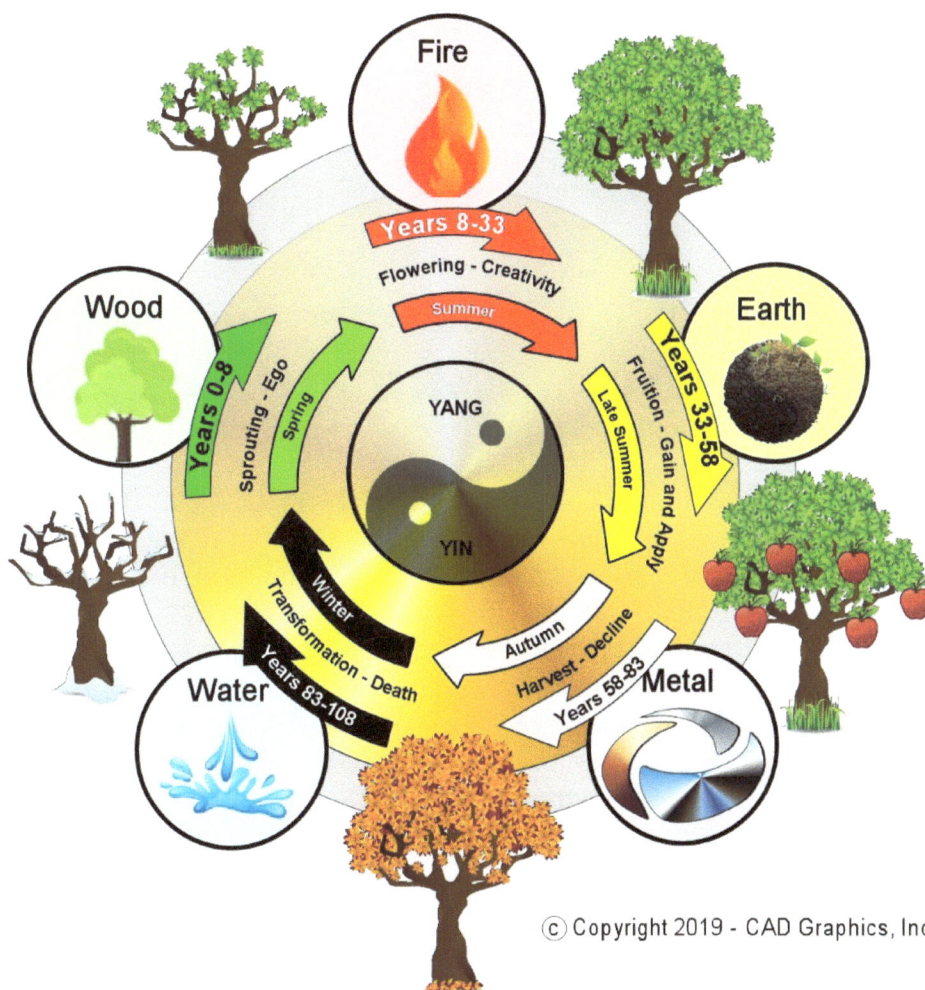

85

Each season or phase has a relationship with one of the 5 elements:

- Spring - Wood - Sprouting 0-8 years old
- Summer - Fire - Flowering 8-33
- Late Summer - Earth - Fruition 33-58
- Autumn - Metal - Harvest 58-83
- Winter - Water - Transformation 83-108

- Some of these relationships might seem somewhat obvious as children have a sprouting or growing personality learning and showing their identity and ego from 0-8 years of age.

- A person from 8-33 is seen as flowering or showing their creativity, intelligence, attractiveness and excessive behavior.

- The 33-58 phase is the fruition years where one starts to blossom as an adult using their knowledge and experience to further their career, family and material assets.

- 58-83 brings the harvest of what was nurtured or squandered from the previous years become more apparent. Health issues arrive if prior neglect is not addressed.

- The last season of transformation from 83-108 is a reflection on what was accomplished mentally, physically and spiritually throughout the prior phases. The realization of self and that the material possessions are only temporary up to this point.

Most people are looking for some type of balance and harmony within their lives. Often, they have no plan nor method to achieve this other than doing their best on a day-to-day basis to find happiness. The 5 Element Theory represents ancient wisdom that when studied and applied, can help to find the balance we seek.

Ancient Chinese scholars of the time approximately from 1600-1000 BC, recognized continuous patterns of change and transformation. Initially, these patterns were interpreted using yin-yang (balance) logic, but later these interpretations were expanded to the theory called The Five Elements. The 5 Elements Theory is based on observation, contemplation and meditation of the natural world and the environment we exist within.

A deeper understanding of these concepts and cycles leads to a more detailed interpretation of these stages into the phases of Warrior - Scholar - Sage. This concept could apply towards many paths in life, where someone starts out more physically involved maturing into more knowledge of a subject and eventually gaining wisdom by understanding how to utilize the knowledge best for a given situation. Examples would be that of a doctor, carpenter, teacher, parent, martial artist - among thousands of other paths on which one gathers knowledge and wisdom through the course of study and practice.

In the martial arts and energetic studies community, the warrior phase relates to *Jing* or the understanding of the essence of the physical body. The scholar phase reflects an understanding of *Chi* or the breath and internal energy flow within the human body. The sage phase is where the experience and knowledge of the previous phases manifests into *Shen* which is one's spirit and self-awareness. The following graphic represents these concepts:

5 Stages of Life
(the 5 element theory)

After the 1st cycle of 0-8 years, each color segment represents 5 years of a 25 year cycle. Each 5 years in turn represents a phase of Spring, Summer, Late Summer, Autumn and Winter.

5 years   25 years

Each 5 years segment has the 5 elements for each year of the cycle: Spring, Summer, Late Summer, Autumn and Winter.

1 year

Spring
Summer
Late Summer
Autumn
Winter

Spring   Summer   Late Summer   Autumn   Winter

Years 8-33

Warrior Years
Jing - move the body
Flowering - Creativity

Summer

Years 0-8

Child Years
Sprouting - Ego

Spring

Years 33-58

Scholar Years
Chi - standing exercises
Fruition - Gain and Apply

Late Summer

FIRE
heart
small
intestine

Creation

Creation

WOOD
liver
gall
bladder

Controls

Controls

EARTH
spleen
stomach

Controls

Controls

WATER
kidneys
bladder

METAL
lungs
lg. intestine

Creation

Creation

Winter

Transformation - Death

Autumn

Harvest - Decline
Shen - still sitting exercises
Sage Years

Immortal - Live or Die

Years 83-108

Years 58-83

Spring

Winter   Autumn   Late Summer

"The Fourth Turning" by William Strauss and Neil Howe articulates a generational theory of history. The authors posit that societies undergo recurring cycles, referred to as "turnings," approximately every 80-100 years. These cycles consist of four distinct generational archetypes of the Prophet, the Nomad, the Hero, and the Artist. Each archetype plays a significant role in shaping and responding to historical events in predictable patterns.
The four *turnings* are:

The High – A period of societal rebuilding after a crisis, characterized by strong institutions, collective unity, and optimism (e.g., post-WWII boom in the U.S.).

The Awakening – A cultural period where individuals challenge established norms, emphasizing personal and spiritual values over conformity (e.g., the 1960s counterculture movement).

The Unraveling – Institutions weaken, individualism increases, and trust in government and societal structures declines (e.g., 1980s-2000s in the U.S.).

The Crisis (Fourth Turning) – Significant upheaval, such as war, economic downturns, or revolution, that forces society to reconstruct itself (e.g., the Great Depression and WWII).

Howe/Strauss Generational Archetypes and Generations

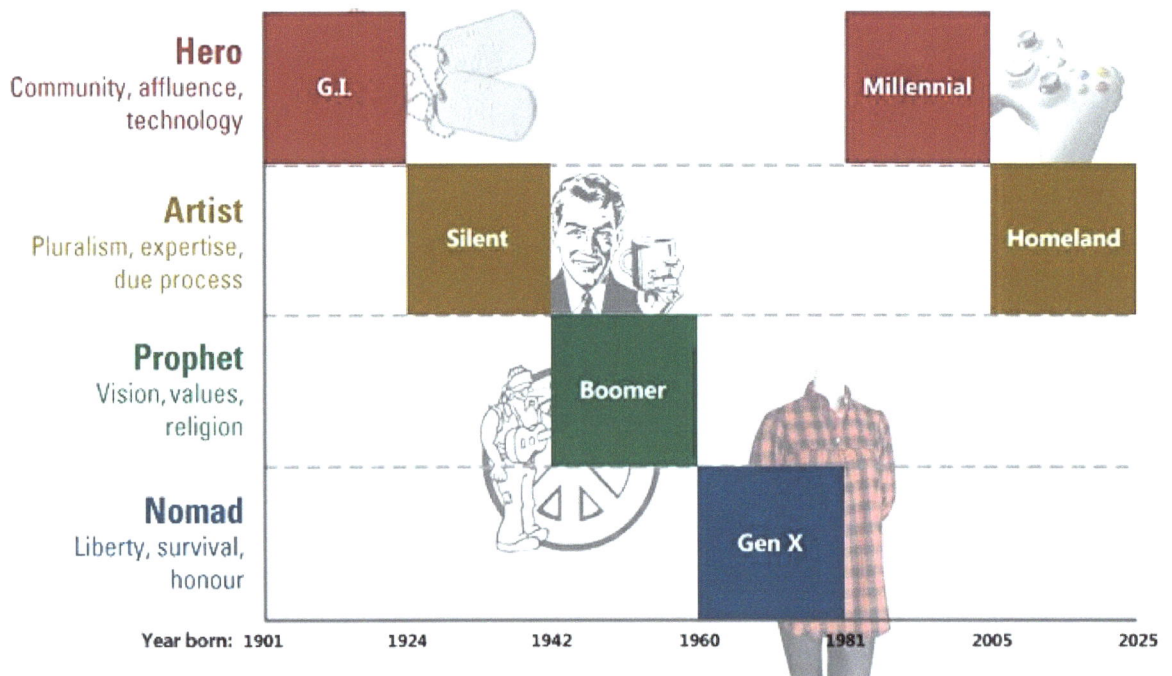

According to their theory, the U.S. is currently in a Fourth Turning (beginning around 2008), indicating we're in a period of crisis and transformation that will likely peak in the 2020s before leading into a new High. William Strauss and Neil Howe's generational theory primarily focuses on Western historical cycles. They did not explicitly incorporate Eastern philosophies like Taoism or the Wu Xing (Five Elements) into their framework. Their analysis centers on patterns observed in Anglo-American history, detailing a recurring cycle of four generational archetypes of Prophet, Nomad, Hero, and Artist, each influencing societal moods and events over approximately 80-100 years.

The Wu Xing in Taoist philosophy describes five interrelated elements of Wood, Fire, Earth, Metal, and Water, each associated with specific seasons, times of day, and life phases. This system emphasizes balance and the dynamic interactions between elements, reflecting the cyclical nature of the universe.

While both frameworks recognize cyclical patterns, their foundations differ: the Wu Xing is rooted in natural elements and their interactions, whereas the Strauss-Howe theory is based on generational dynamics and historical events. There isn't direct evidence that Strauss and Howe studied or integrated Eastern philosophies into their work.

Carl Jung, a Swiss psychiatrist and psychoanalyst, introduced the idea of psychological archetypes and was significantly influenced by his study of Eastern philosophies. Jung's incorporation of concepts from Taoism, Buddhism, and other Eastern traditions into his work on the collective unconscious and archetypes predated the Strauss-Howe generational theory by decades. While Strauss and Howe developed their own unique framework focused on historical and generational patterns, the notion of archetypes they used resonates with the broader tradition of exploring recurring patterns in human behavior and culture.

However, the concept of cyclical patterns is present in many cultural philosophies, suggesting a universal human inclination to find order and predictability in history and nature. While the specifics of the cycles differ between the Wu Xing and the Strauss-Howe generational theory, both offer perspectives on understanding the rhythms and transformations inherent in societies.

Universal Cycles of Transformation

Each framework describes a repeating sequence of phases, with distinct yet interrelated roles:

- **Strauss & Howe's** *Fourth Turning* follows a **four-phase** generational cycle (~80-100 years), where societal moods shift from stability (*High*) to questioning (*Awakening*), fragmentation (*Unraveling*), and renewal through crisis (*Crisis*).

- **Wu Xing (Five Elements)** describes a **five-phase** natural cycle (Wood, Fire, Earth, Metal, Water), applied to time, seasons, and human life. Taoism sees a person's lifespan in ~25-year segments: **0-8 (Spring), 8-33 (Summer), 33-58 (Late Summer), 58-83 (Autumn), and 83-108 (Winter)**—closely mirroring *The Fourth Turning's* phases.

- **Jungian Archetypes** reflect psychological transformations across an individual's life and history. His concepts of *Hero, Wise Old Man, Shadow, and Rebirth* mirror the rise, crisis, and renewal patterns seen in the other two theories. Jung, influenced by Taoism and the *I Ching*, recognized life as a process of individuation—balancing opposing forces (Yin-Yang, conscious-unconscious), much like the generational and elemental cycles.

Seasons of Life - 5 Elements

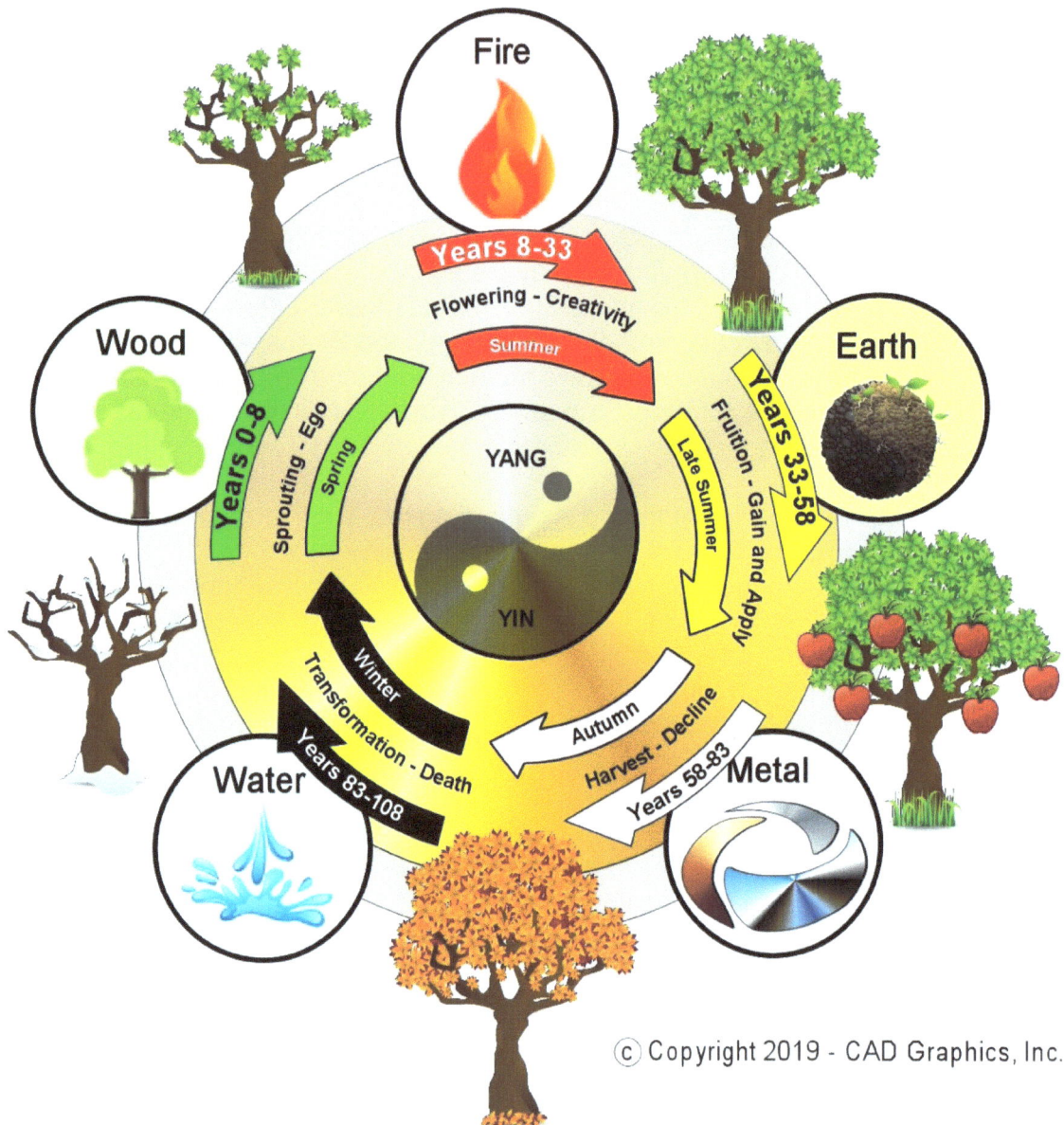

© Copyright 2019 - CAD Graphics, Inc.

Carl Jung's Other Archetypes: Recurring Roles in Human Experience

Carl Jung believed that "archetypes" are fundamental patterns (instincts) that are found within the collective unconscious that express universal aspects of human experiences. An archetype is an original pattern or model from which all things of the same kind are copied or based upon, essentially a perfect example or prototype that serves as the foundation for other similar things. There are as many archetypes as there are typical situations found in everyday life. Many of the most powerful ideas have that have been repeated throughout history, lead back to archetypes.

yin and yang can be found in all things

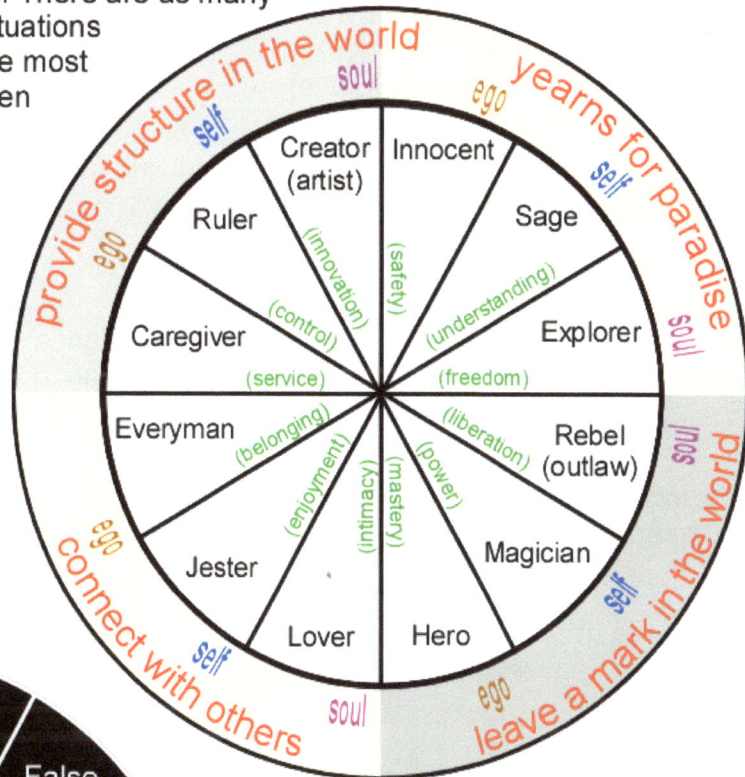

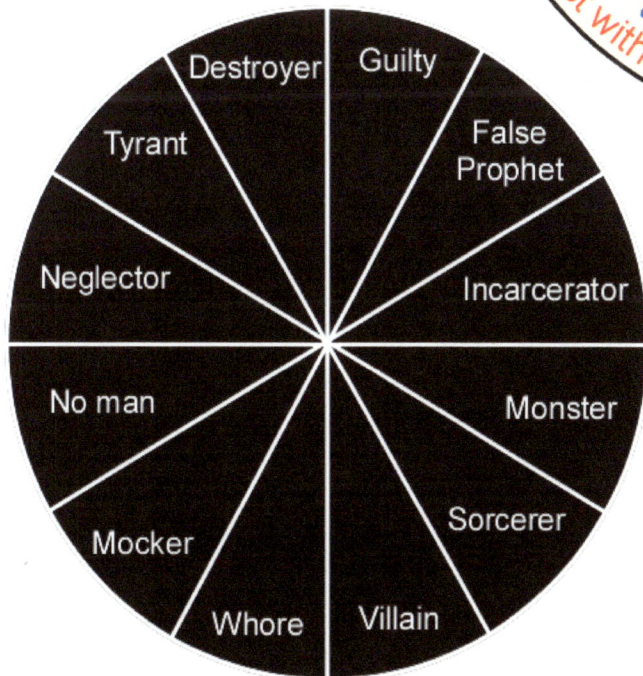

Comparison of The Fourth Turning, Wu Xing (Five Elements), and Jungian Archetypes

Aspect	The Fourth Turning (Strauss & Howe)	Wu Xing (Five Elements - Taoism)	Carl Jung's Archetypes & Eastern Influence
Core Concept	Generational cycles shaping historical events	Cycles of transformation in nature and human life	Universal psychological patterns shaping human experience
Number of Phases	4 (High, Awakening, Unraveling, Crisis)	5 (Wood, Fire, Earth, Metal, Water)	Multiple archetypes (Self, Shadow, Anima/Animus, Wise Old Man, Hero, etc.)
Time Cycle	~80-100 years per full cycle (each turning lasts ~20-25 years)	Life follows a ~100-year cycle: 0-8 (Spring), 8-33 (Summer), 33-58 (Late Summer), 58-83 (Autumn), 83-108 (Winter)	Archetypes manifest across an individual's life and society's evolution, influencing cultural narratives
Driving Force	Generational archetypes influencing societal shifts	Dynamic balance of natural elements influencing change	Unconscious patterns and symbols shaping human behavior
Pattern of Change	Crisis leads to rebirth and restructuring	Elements generate or control each other, creating harmony or conflict	Archetypes emerge in different life-stages and cultural epochs
Examples in History	WWII as a Fourth Turning crisis leading to a post-war High	Wood (spring) symbolizes growth, Metal (autumn) signifies decline	Myths and symbols across cultures share common archetypal themes
Application	Political, social, and economic shifts	Medicine (TCM), philosophy, astrology, martial arts, feng shui	Psychology, mythology, dream analysis, philosophy, and cultural studies
Influence on Individuals	People shaped by generational identity	Individuals follow natural life phases: childhood, vitality, maturity, reflection, and transformation	Archetypes guide personal development and collective human experiences
Philosophical Foundation	Western historical analysis	Taoist metaphysics and observation of nature	Jung was deeply influenced by Taoism, Buddhism, and alchemy, integrating these into his theories
View on Crisis & Renewal	Crisis (Fourth Turning) is inevitable but leads to rebirth	Destruction and transformation are necessary for balance	Individuation process—integrating the unconscious with the

Aspect	The Fourth Turning (Strauss & Howe)	Wu Xing (Five Elements - Taoism)	Carl Jung's Archetypes & Eastern Influence
			conscious—requires facing inner conflicts

Key Takeaways:

1. **Generational, Natural, and Psychological Patterns Are Interwoven**
   - Each theory observes cyclical phases that repeat over time, whether in **history (Fourth Turning), nature (Wu Xing), or the psyche (Jungian archetypes).**

   - Crisis and renewal are fundamental to change, whether societal, elemental, or personal.

2. **Strauss & Howe's Generational Theory May Unconsciously Reflect Jungian Archetypes**
   - *The Fourth Turning's* generational archetypes (Prophet, Nomad, Hero, Artist) resemble Jung's archetypal roles.

   - Jung, who studied Taoism and Eastern philosophy, recognized cycles of transformation, much like *Wu Xing's* elemental shifts.

3. **Taoism's Wu Xing and Jung's Individuation Both Emphasize Balance**
   - *Wu Xing* describes the dynamic interplay of elements, where excess in one leads to transformation into another.

   - Jung's individuation process requires integrating all aspects of the psyche, much like how Taoist balance ensures harmony.

4. **Crisis is a Necessary Stage for Renewal**
   - *Fourth Turning:* Each crisis (e.g., WWII) paves the way for societal rebirth.

   - *Wu Xing:* Death and decay (Metal & Water) are necessary before new life (Wood).

   - *Jung:* Transformation only occurs when the individual faces their *Shadow* and integrates unconscious aspects.

Though emerging from different traditions, these three theories reveal a shared truth: transformation occurs through cyclical forces, shaping societies, nature, and individuals alike. Whether through generational change, elemental shifts, or psychological evolution, the rhythm of crisis and renewal is an eternal pattern in human experience.

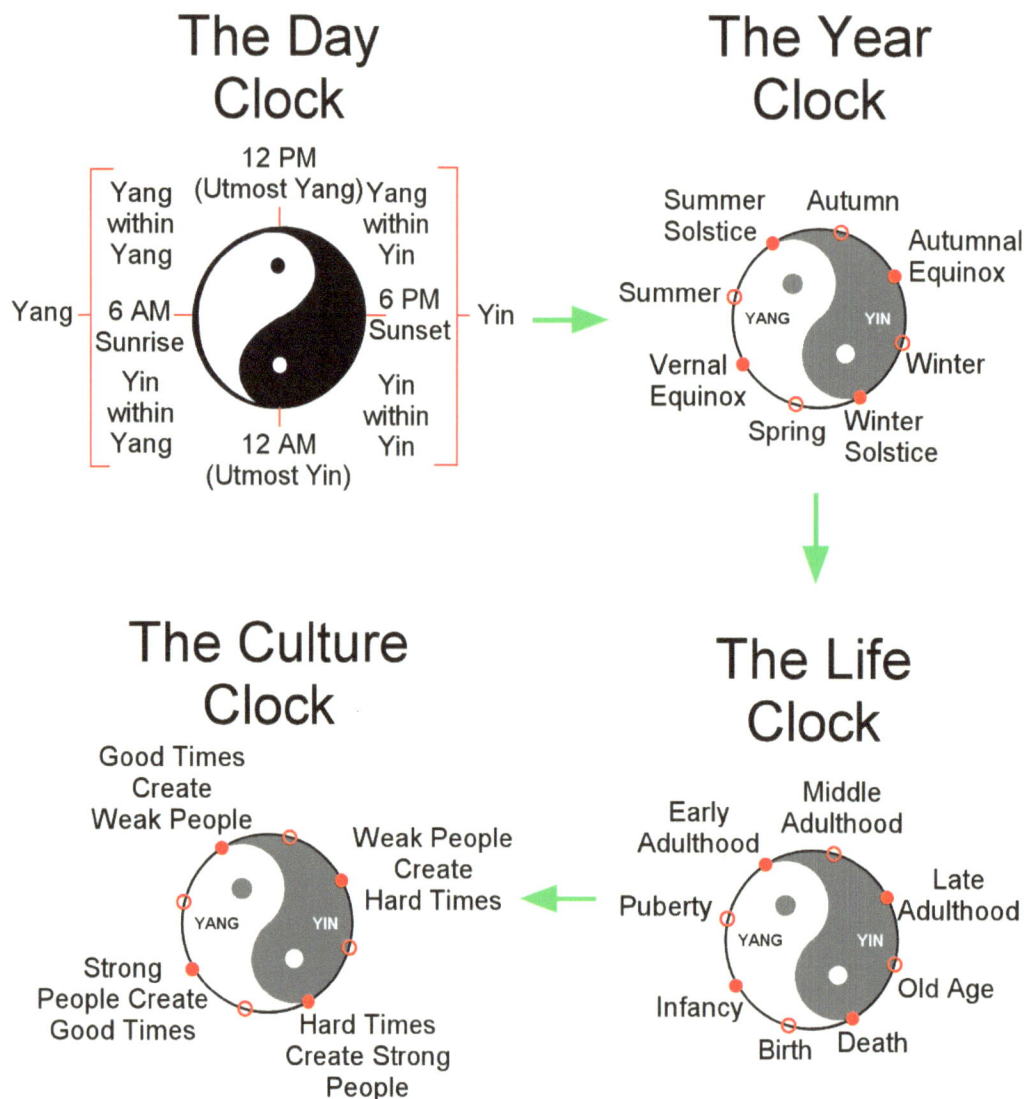

The Day Clock

12 PM
(Utmost Yang)

Yang within Yang

Yang within Yin

Yang

6 AM Sunrise

6 PM Sunset

Yin

Yin within Yang

Yin within Yin

12 AM
(Utmost Yin)

The Year Clock

Summer Solstice

Autumn

Autumnal Equinox

Summer

YANG

YIN

Vernal Equinox

Winter

Spring

Winter Solstice

The Culture Clock

Good Times Create Weak People

Weak People Create Hard Times

YANG

YIN

Strong People Create Good Times

Hard Times Create Strong People

The Life Clock

Early Adulthood

Middle Adulthood

Late Adulthood

Puberty

YANG

YIN

Infancy

Old Age

Birth

Death

"Hard times create strong men. Strong men create good times. Good times create weak men. And weak men create hard times." — G. Michael Hopf,

References:

Generations X u Y: Crux, Characteristics, Application of a Theory in Recruiting. (2023). https://itluckyhunter.com/blog/generations-theory

The 3 Treasures - Mind, Body & Spirit

The most valuable things that we all possess. Without these 3, we have no family, no friends, no career, no big house, no internet.

We all need to take care of our own "treasures" before we can be of benefit to those around us. Breathe deeper, exercise more, eat better, earn a good night's sleep by being active and relieving stress during the day. Just sharing what has been known for a very long time; these are universal truths that are hard to debate.

Mind — Qi (Energy) 氣

Body — Jing (Essence) 精

Spirit — Shen (spirit) 神

The Foundation - the 3 Treasures

www.MindAndBodyExercises.com

© Copyright 2024 - CAD Graphics, Inc.

The 5 Element Theory - Various Manifestations

Ancient Chinese scholars from thousands of years ago, recognized continuous patterns of change and transformation of natural cycles within the world and its environments that we exist in. The simple explanation can be distilled down to the fact that basically everything we know exists, in a delicate balance where each component affects every other component.

Not as basic, was how these patterns were interpreted using yin-yang (balance & harmony) logic. Later these interpretations were expanded to become somewhat more complex and called The Five Phase Theory (Wu Xing) or the Five Element Theory. The 5 Phase Theory is based on observation, contemplation, and meditation upon these various cycles and their processes, functions, and phenomena of nature and inner relationships with one another.

The theory proclaims that aspects of matter can be divided into one of five basic elements of wood, fire, earth, metal, and water. Each element contains their own specific characteristics and interrelationships. In modern times, the Five Phase Theory is still used as a tool for grouping substances and structures, as well as a method for studying changes of natural phenomena related to health and disease.

One of the more obvious cycles is that of the change of climatic seasons from one to the next, initiating from the Earth's yearly revolution around the Sun. Each season has a corresponding element as well as a relative balance of yin and yang. Spring spouts like growing plants (wood), Summer brings warmth (fire), late Summer brings maturation (earth), Fall brings the harvest (metal) while Winter brings transformation of death and rebirth (water). Just as these seasons affect the earth, so is plant and animal life affected.

The 5 Phase Theory is a major component of thought within TCM or traditional Chinese medicine. These elements have corresponding relationships within our environment as well as within our own being specifically the internal organs and emotions connected to them.

Most people are looking for some type of balance and harmony within their lives. Often, they have no plan nor method to achieve this other than doing their best on a day-to-day basis to find happiness. The 5 Phase Theory represents ancient wisdom that when studied and applied, can help to find the balance we seek.

The following graphic shows the simplicity progressing to the complexity of this concept.

Wu Xing Various Manifestations

The 5 Element Theory
(Wu Xing)

www.MindAndBodyExercises.com

The 5 Element Theory
(creation & control cycles)

www.MindAndBodyExercises.com

The 5 Element Theory
(internal organ pairings)

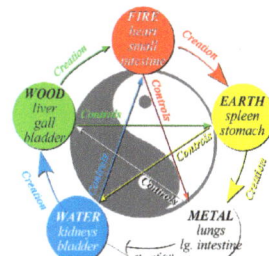

www.MindAndBodyExercises.com

The 5 Elements
(emotions affect organs)

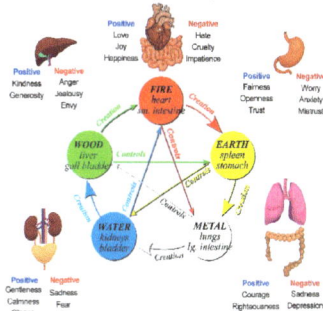

www.MindAndBodyExercises.com

The 5 Shen
(spirits of the consciousness)

www.MindAndBodyExercises.com

The 5 Seasons of Life
(the 5 element theory)

www.MindAndBodyExercises.com

5 Stages of Life
(the 5 element theory)

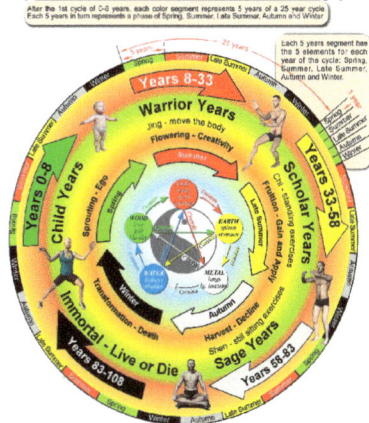

www.MindAndBodyExercises.com

The 5 Element Theory
(and introduction of the 6th element)

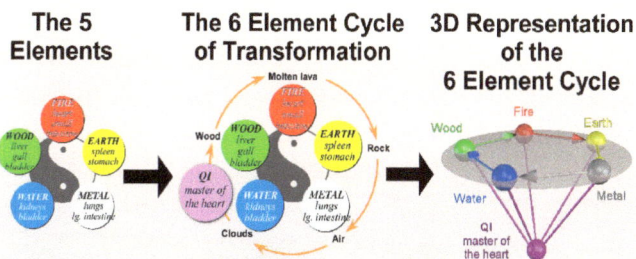

www.MindAndBodyExercises.com

The Greatest Gift You Can Give is a Healthy You

Gifts like diamonds, iPhones, clothes, and maybe even food on the table, all might be very nice and thoughtful gifts. But really, ... let's get real. Time with those you love and care about is priceless. How can someone spend time with another when they are not healthy enough to be alive in the first place? Or, if one's life is consumed with managing one's own ailments, the consequences of poor health and well-being may affect all in their presence.

While it may seem selfish to put your own health and well-being first, it is actually the most giving of oneself to be a living vessel of love, compassion and knowledge to those around you, for as long as possible.

My understanding is that **you can only give out what you yourself have an abundance of.**

A HEALTHY **YOU** IS THE **GREATEST GIFT YOU CAN GIVE YOUR FAMILY.**

SON   FATHER

Soldiers, law enforcement officers, firefighters and others need to be in good physical, as well as mental health if they are to be of service in protecting and preserving human life. Similar to emergency room doctors, nurses and others that can find themselves very run down or ill, while attempting to treat patients. Others may be a parent taking care of a child, a caretaker of a parent, teachers, etc. It is all about intent and energy expelled and received. One individual loses some level of energy while trying to help another. When we continue to draw from our well (life force, qi, prana) but fail to replenish it, we will soon have our own health issues. Exercise, diet, stress management, attitude, and other lifestyle choices all affect our own well-being to replenish or retain our innate life force.

Health Management

I have found (and teach) the following methods to be extremely beneficial for many people, regardless of age or current health conditions:

- Diaphragmatic breathing
- Progressive muscle relaxation
- Guided imagery
- Mindfulness
- Physical activity
- Limiting exposure to triggers
- Mind and body exercises such as yoga

The Meaning of the 8 Trigrams and Bagua

The following is a very basic explanation of the Meaning of the 8 Trigrams and Bagua. There are many books and resources that go into greater depth regarding these ancient concepts of balance and harmony.

The four phases that are generated by the two poles (yin pole, yang pole) are represented by Metal, Wood, Water and Fire. They also assume the manifestation of four strengths: greater yang, lesser yang, greater yin and lesser yin. The four phases yield the eight trigrams. Heaven-Lion, Earth-Unicorn, Thunder-Dragon, Wind-Phoenix, Water-Snake, Fire-Hawk, Mountain-Bear and Lake-Monkey. The Zhou Yi also represented the above derivation with symbols. The straight line represents the Yang phase, and a broken line represents the Yin phase.

The following diagrams will help you see the progression of the development of the Eight Trigrams.

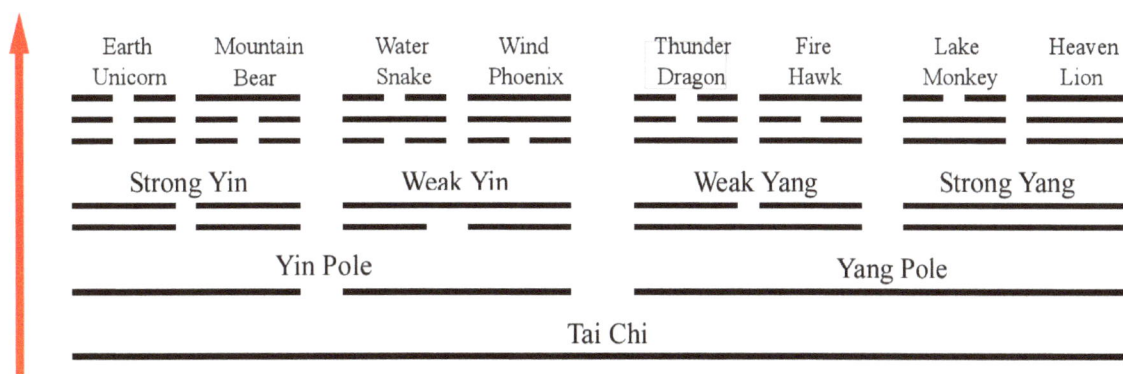

This concept then translates into the graphical representation of the bagua, or eight-sided figure as shown below.

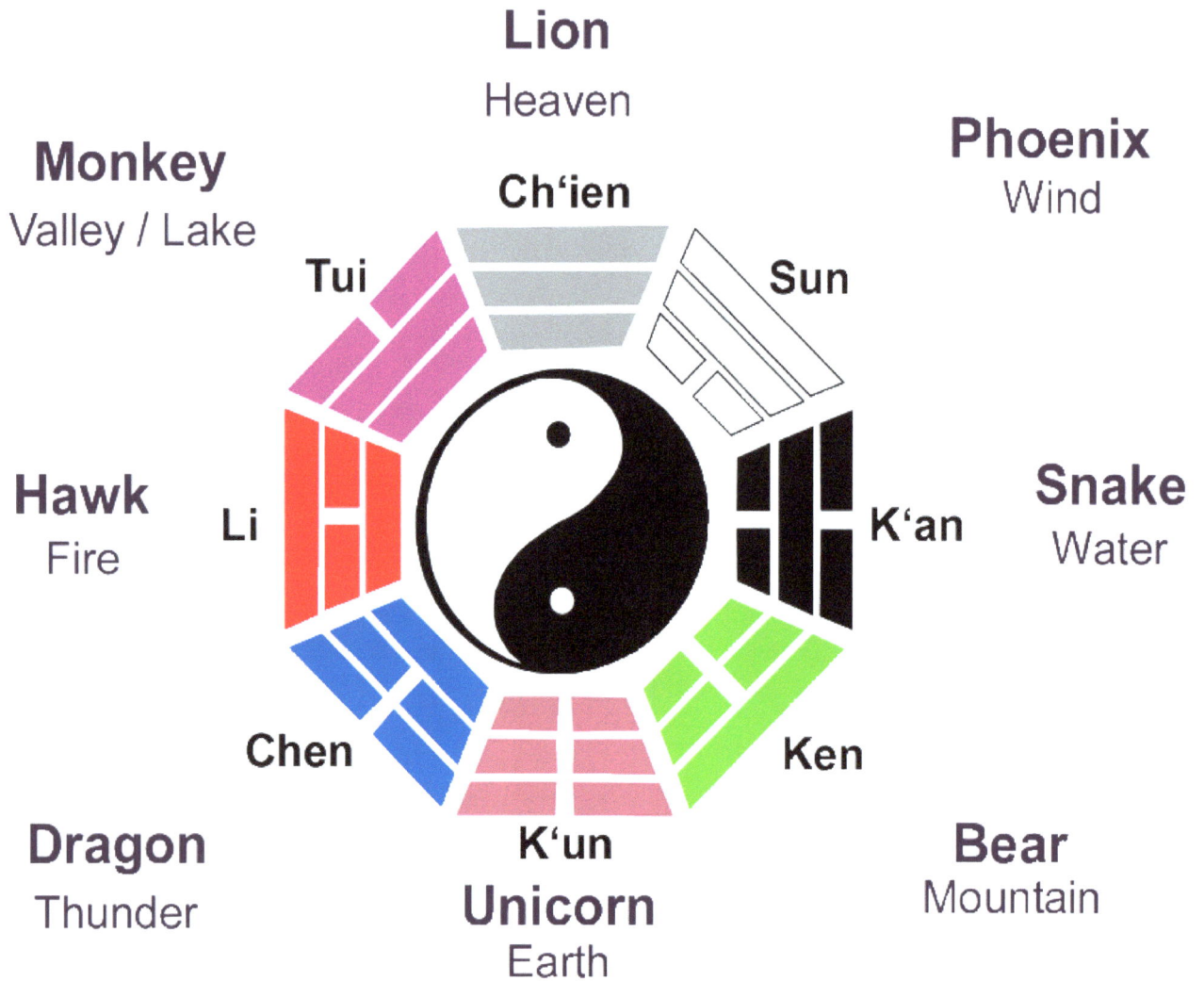

Lion
Heaven
Ch'ien

Monkey
Valley / Lake
Tui

Phoenix
Wind
Sun

Hawk
Fire
Li

Snake
Water
K'an

Dragon
Thunder
Chen

Unicorn
Earth
K'un

Bear
Mountain
Ken

www.MindandBodyExercises.com

The yin and yang symbol or taijitu, relates to the day and night association of yin and yang. Supposedly the ancients plotted a graph made up of six concentrically larger rings. In the center anchored an 8-foot-high pole that measured the shadow cast by the sun throughout the seasons. Then they colored where the shade landed and where there was none. When looked at from above, the graph showed a picture that resembles the yin and yang symbol but without the two dots on either side. From here the concept of balance and its relationship to the seasons and nature was conceived.

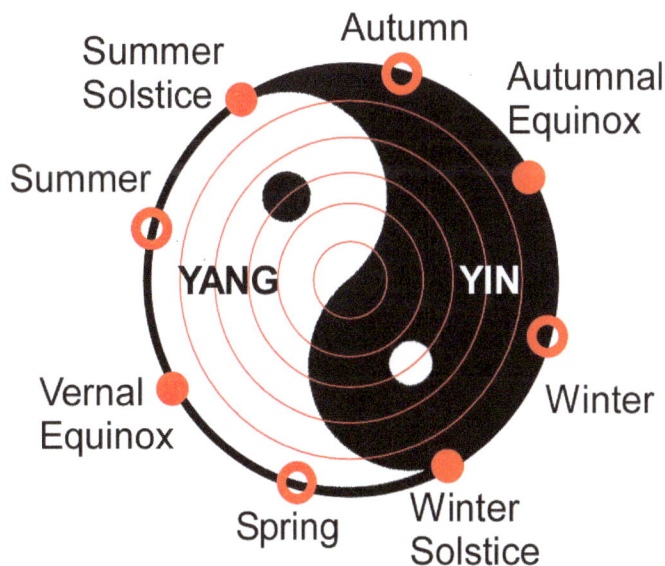

© Copyright 2020 - CAD Graphics, Inc.

The yin-yang symbol has been long known to represent balance and harmony. However, some choose to label it as a religious symbol for Daoism which many consider more of a

101

philosophy. The martial art of tai chi uses this symbol and concept as a foundation to understand the flow of energy within the human body.

The 5 Aspects of yin and yang complement and balance each other via these aspects, which define the relationship between each.

The Five Aspects of Yin and Yang

The 5 Aspects of yin and yang complement and balance each other via these aspects, which define the relationship between each.

1) Opposition

2) Interdependence

3) Mutual Consuming-Increasing

4) Mutual Transforming

5) Infinite Divisibility

www.MindAndBodyExercises.com

Mind - Body - Spirit

Often times we hear of the mind, body and spirit harmony expressed in the news, at the health club, yoga studio, coffee shops or places of worship. Spirituality and religion are often lumped together but have rather distinctly different meanings. So, let's look at spiritually more as a level of self-awareness, purpose and life direction and not necessarily a membership to any particular religion or belief system.

Who doesn't desire a strong, sharp and intelligent mind?

A healthy, strong and disease-free body to last us into our latter years of life would also be nice.

A strong connection to a higher power gives us direction, a hope for something greater than ourselves and for some sense of purpose.

A Balanced Life - One Perspective

Mind

Intent
Intellect
Inner dialogue
Positive attitude
Personal boundaries
Emotion management

Body

Physical health
Proper nutrition
Adequate sleep
Personal hygiene
Stress management
Exercise and movement
Responsible medical care
Preservation of resources

Spirit

Self-awareness
Values & morals
Sense of purpose
Seeing yourself, as others see you
Faith in something bigger than yourself

103

A harmony between the mind, body and spirit would wrap it all in a nice package, right? But how does this come about other than merely saying that this is what I am pursuing? I work out daily, go to church regularly, eat healthy foods, read books and magazines, stay informed - I have the *mind, body and mind connection* down pat, right? I guess it depends on what my goals and expectations are relative to achieving this harmony.

To pursue a strong, disciplined and intelligent mind, I think one needs to become and stay educated. Whether from schooling, reading, employment, life experiences, etc. you need to keep learning as long as you are able to. Once you think you know all of any particular subject matter, you limit yourself to learning something new or experiencing a different perspective of whatever knowledge you may already understand.

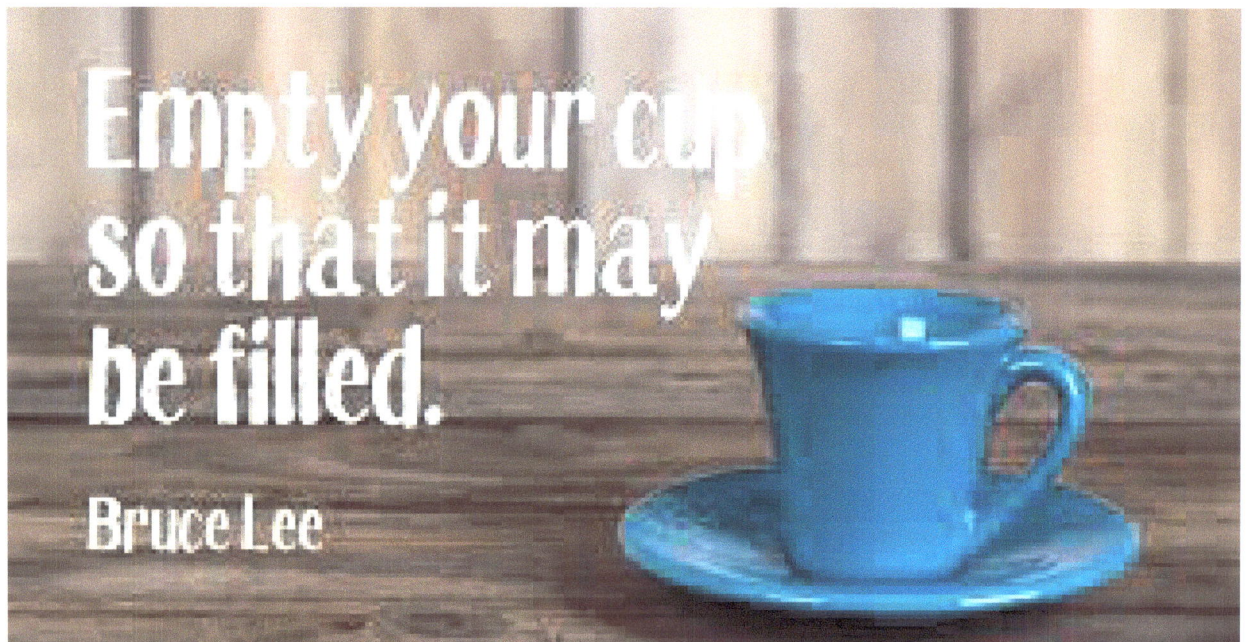

Empty your cup so that it may be filled.

Bruce Lee

To achieve a healthy and disease-free body, usually requires some amount of physical effort or restraint from activities that tear the body down or put oneself in bodily harm or injury. Very few people make it past the middle ages of 33-58, free of injury or disease if they are not aware of what they eat, how they move their body (whether for career, fitness or lifestyle) and what they focus their thoughts upon. Thoughts being positive, happy, optimistic or more negative, depressed, counterproductive.

Acquiring a strong spirit doesn't necessarily require attending religious institutions or services, but for many it provides the direction or path to do so. Others go directly to the source, but I feel to each their own as long as it doesn't infringe upon others living their lives and enjoying their freedoms to do so. I do however think that some method of self-reflection needs to be cultivated in order to see oneself as others see them. With this awareness, one can pursue the best version of their self, as a daily practice and not an occasional event.

Methods for Self-reflection

1 - Observation
2 - Contemplation
3 - Mediation
4 - Prayer

Engaging the mind to become the observer of one's thoughts

There are many methods and formulas to achieve the mind, body and spirit connection I am writing about. In this article forward, I am referring more towards yoga, tai chi, qigong and martial arts practices. These I am most familiar with from my studying, practicing and teaching of for almost 40 years.

I feel that much of the yoga, qigong, tai chi and martial arts, being currently taught in the United States to the general public through health clubs, wellness centers, community rec centers, etc. is a watered-down version of these practices focusing merely on fitness and sometimes some other health aspects such as flexibility and stress relief. Many wellness centers try to fill up their calendars to offer the "one stop shop" featuring every version of fitness available. Spin classes, water aerobics, personal training, meditation, jazzercise, and the alternatives like yoga and tai chi - you name it, they will provide it. Often times the instructors are exercise instructors or ones who have picked up a weekend course on a particular subject, who are now "qualified" to teach the methods without much really diligent practical experience themselves.

All You Can Attend Exercise Buffet

- yoga   - tai chi

- pilates   - qigong

- meditation   - cardio kung fu

99¢ per person, no sharing please

All of these methods can be taught or practiced as "yoga-light", "tai chi-easy" or "cardio-kung fu" but the reality is that it takes time, physical effort and deliberate thought to achieve beyond the basic fitness benefits. Current culture doesn't really encourage individuals to join the yoga ashram nor retreat into the mountains for years of training and isolation.

What took years of physical training, observation, contemplation and meditation in years past, is now packaged in weekend seminars or 200 or 500-hour programs that take a few months to a year or two to become "certified". This is great that so many more people have more access to what was previously kept to yogis, monks and royalty. Those that are more

106

knowledgeable or good teachers usually move on to have their own clients or businesses elsewhere.

What is being left out is the actual mind and body integration that can lead to the higher levels of self-healing, chronic pain management and self-awareness. One will find it difficult to achieve a better understanding of self when they are not challenged to self-critique the inner dialogue that is part of the human condition. These aspects are not currently acceptable as mainstream within fitness centers, as it delves into asking the individual to question their own reality and look into the mirror to maybe see something they don't care to deal with.

It is interesting though that the practices previously mentioned were indeed originally developed as a means of self-preservation of the body and mind to unite with their spirit. Yoga means "yoke" or "unite." The yogi greeting of "namaste", may the god in me see the god in you. Kung Fu meaning "hard" or "deliberate" work. Tai Chi means "the supreme ultimate". Qigong means "energy" or "life force" work. You get the idea, being a deeper meaning or purpose behind the names themselves. Currently, yoga is often looked upon as glorified yuppie stretching; you have to have the yoga pants (I prefer Lululemon), the Hydro Flask water bottle. Tai chi is commonly perceived as exercise for old people who can't run. And qigong, well that is weird mediation and chanting stuff, right? Most people don't want to spend the time to become better educated about these methods but would rather do the yoga-stretching classes at the gym, lift some weights, bike or run to feel the "burn", break the sweat or overall, just feel like physical exertion is the means to get in touch with their inner self.

Please don't misunderstand my frustration with pursuing only the physical benefits of training. The physical training and self-discipline is indeed the gateway to a better understanding and management of ones thoughts and emotions. By disciplining the body, this leads to disciplining the thoughts and breathing rhythms which can consequently lead to higher levels of self-awareness.

There are still some very good teachers and schools/centers that continue to teach the mind/body/spirit aspects; but one needs to seek them out. Their numbers are dwindling, and there is the real possibility that the deeper root of knowledge will not be passed on to the next generations unless in books, videos or other resources. Supply and demand. No demand from people wanting to learn about the value of the mind, body and spirit connection, means the supply of teachers will continue to decline. You can't make people understand the value of a diamond by giving it them for free. One cannot value an education that they did not earn for themselves. Is a college degree worth the paper it is written on, or is the lessons and experience of the education process where the value is ? Teachers cannot pass the knowledge out if the student doesn't desire it to begin with. Knowledge is freedom. The sharing knowledge is when knowledge becomes powerful.

———

Trust or Faith?
The American people have lost their trust (based on what can be seen from actions) in our leaders and experts. Many have lost their faith (beliefs that cannot be physically seen) in people having a moral compass.

Dictionary.com defines 'trust' as:
- Reliance on the integrity, strength, ability, surety, etc., of a person or thing; confidence
- Confident expectation of something; hope
- Confidence in the certainty of future payment for property or goods received; credit: to sell merchandise on trust
- A person on whom or thing on which one relies: God is my trust
- The condition of one to whom something has been entrusted

Dictionary.com defines 'faith' as:
- Confidence or trust in a person or thing
- Belief that is not based on proof
- Belief in God or in the doctrines or teachings of religion
- A system of religious belief
-

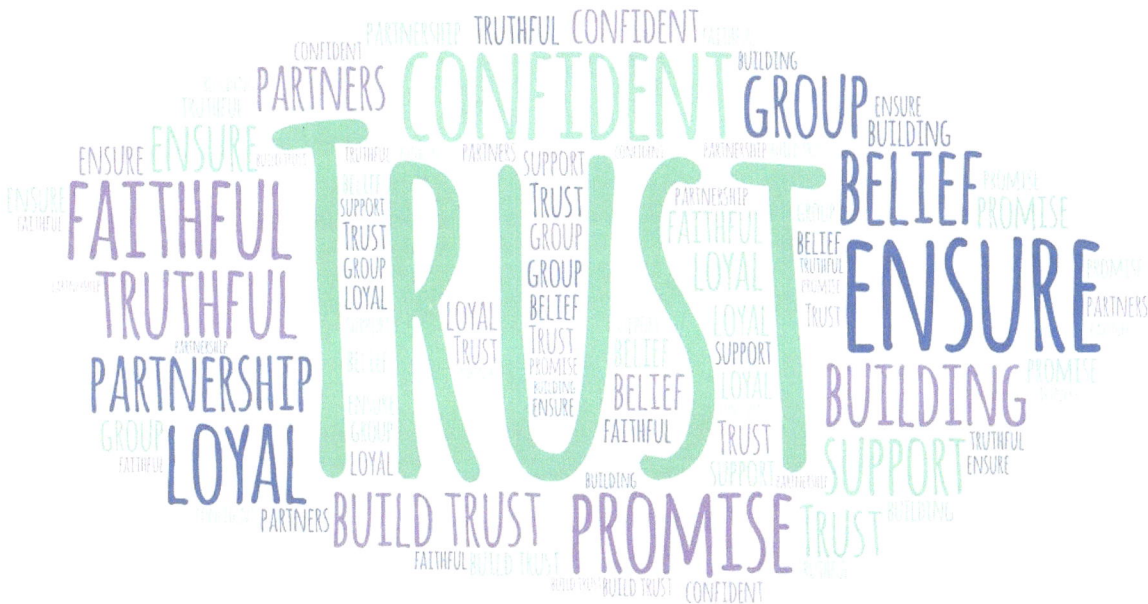

I often see the daily news, on TV or in print and other specials on the current health crisis, but very few report **why** people view things a particular way. For example, why are there a significant number of health care and law enforcement workers refusing to be vaccinated and consequently resigning, retiring early or risk being fired? Reports may say that they have lost trust in the government or the medical community, but why is this so? Why are licensed and long-experienced doctors opposing vaccine mandates, risking their livelihoods and reputations? One answer is long-term effects cannot be determined in the short-term.

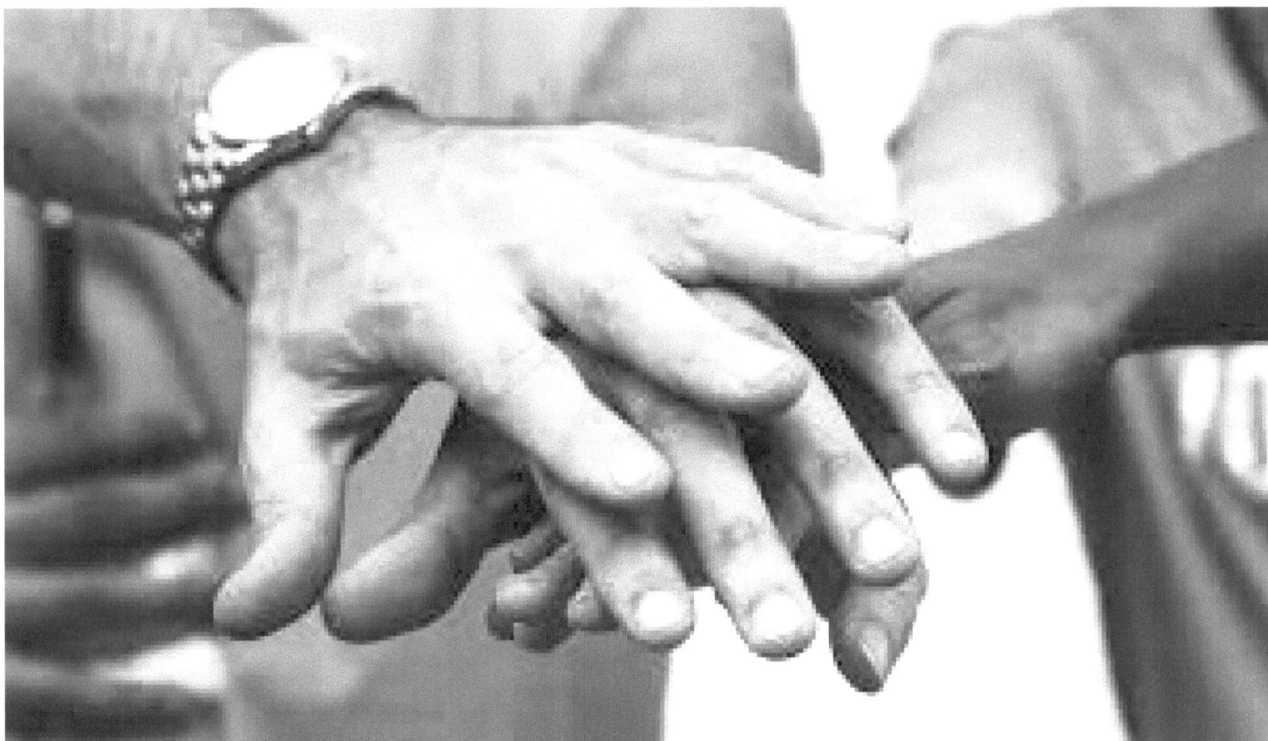

If people are to move in a particular direction that affects the health and well-being of themselves and their loved ones, professionals and leaders need to stop doing things that make some people question these actions. If there is no medical data available yet to support long-term effects of the Covid19 virus nor the relative vaccines, let the public know this and not assume the attitude that people will believe experts if no accurate data is available. I think people would prefer to know the truth even if not good or definitive, rather than feel like the goal post keeps being moved back.

TRUST IS EARNED WHEN ACTIONS MEET WORDS

Professionals that have an audience can start by just putting themselves out there with some transparency, honesty, humility, and empathy regarding these topics at hand. If a physician (Scott Gotlieb) is interviewed as an expert on a particular topic (appearing almost weekly on CBS's Face the Nation), have them tell their story of being a director for the FDA and now being a board member for Pfizer, instead of people Googling this fact, seeing it maybe as a conflict of interest and then formulating their own conspiracy theory from it. Per the Pfizer investors' site, Pfizer reported 2021 second quarter revenues of $19.0 billion, and an operational growth of 86%. For those who think that the vaccines were made free to the public, don't quite understand that Pfizer billed the US government, who then taxes the citizens, who actually paid the $19.0 billion through taxes and loss of other potential investment or purchases.

It is worth noting that Pfizer is a sponsor for the following news media:
Good Morning America
CBS Health Watch
Anderson Cooper 360
ABC News Nightline
Making A Difference
CNN Tonight
Early Start
Erin Burnett Out Front
ABC's This Week With George Stephanopoulos
Good Morning America's Weather Report
Today's Countdown to the Royal Wedding
CBS Sports Update
Meet The Press
CBS This Morning
60 Minutes

Pfizer can be seen as possibly influencing the objectivity of these news outlets, as journalists and reporters might not be as likely to be critical of Pfizer when such powerful companies are spending millions of dollars on advertising during these news shows.

Similarly, if the FDA is going to report that they took 108 days to review documents for licensing of the Pfizer covid19 vaccine and will honor a Freedom of Information Act (FOIA) request, don't take 55 years to fully release the information to the group of scientists that made the request. Stop creating the perfect storm of events that will undoubtedly lead to more conspiracy theories and consequently, more of a lack of trust and faith in leaders and experts having a moral compass.

I think the best way that political leaders as well as medical experts can help is by performing any actions that can help rebuild the trust towards the medical community. Interviews, documentaries, news articles, mailing, or whatever mode of information distribution is embraced, do so with transparency, honesty, humility, and empathy.

Our next healthcare crisis is not that far in the future. I would hope that some have a moral compass that would point towards encouraging people to become healthy and maintain their own well-being before another crisis occurs.

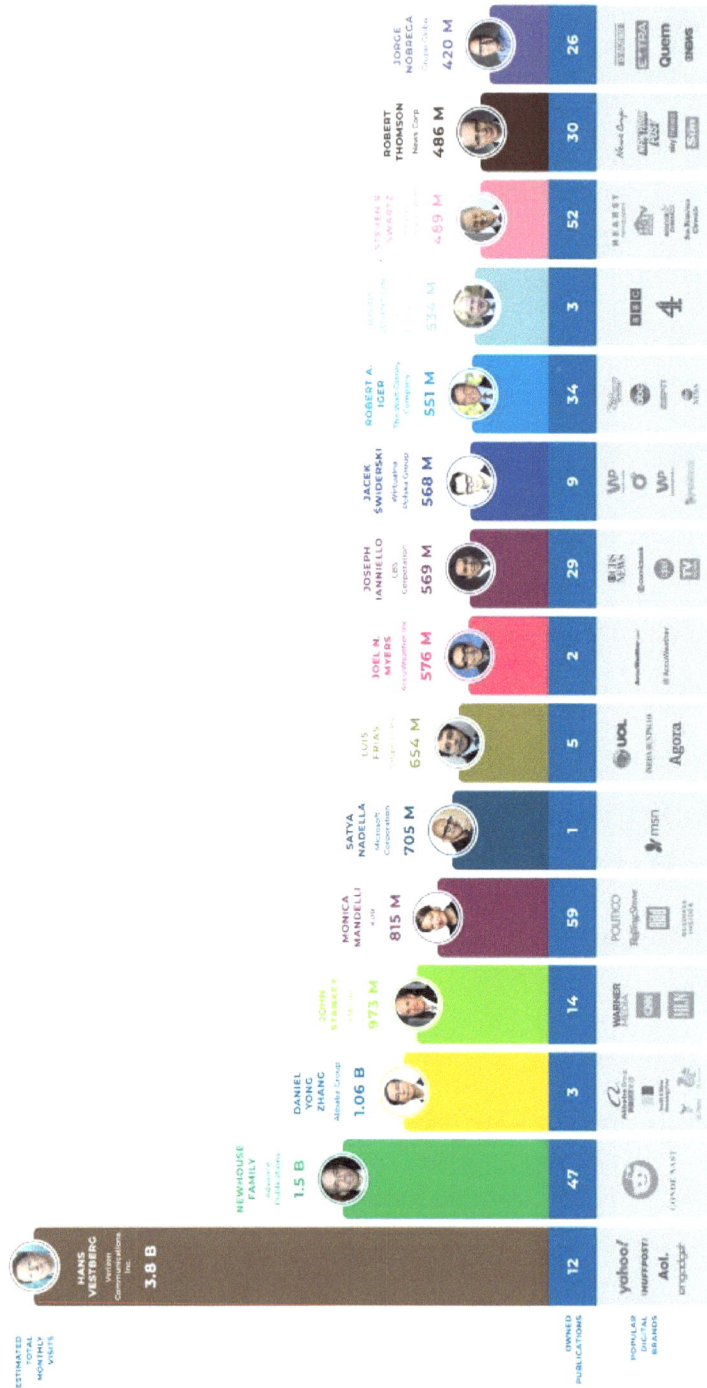

THE WORLD'S MOST POWERFUL MEDIA MOGULS:
Which CEOs have the most influence online?

The media has huge influence over consumer tastes, political opinions, and culture at large, so it's important to know who controls the news we consume every day. This chart ranks CEOs (and their companies) by who has access to the largest online audience, based on SimilarWeb estimated monthly visits for all their web properties.

https://www.addictivetips.com/news/who-owns-the-news/

112

Warrior - Scholar - Sage

3 distinct mindsets and/or phases, when it comes to training and self-improvement. However, this concept can also be applied towards various other walks of life from the soldier. the martial artist, the yoga practitioner, the car mechanic, the nurse, the carpenter, etc.

The Warrior - focuses mostly on the physical, the body, the movement, doing the work, getting the job done, defending, protecting

The Scholar - focuses on the history, the backstory, the mechanics, understanding how, when, where and why things work

The Sage - draws upon the life experiences from being a warrior and/or scholar to making wise decisions

https://youtu.be/FpKpl4XwOcw

The 3 Treasures

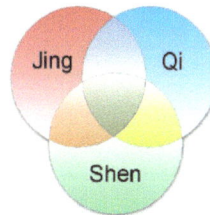

Jing   Qi

Shen

精 **Warrior Phase**
Jing (Essence)

氣 **Scholar Phase**
Qi (Energy)

神 **Sage Phase**
Shen (Spirit)

Be the Warrior, the Scholar, the Sage - a Blueprint to Happiness & Purpose

精

Jing (Essence)

Warrior Phase

Through practicing physical movements (Jing - essence), one can better develop:

1) Awareness – realization, perception or knowledge

2) Memory – the process of reproducing or recalling what has been learned or experienced

3) Coordination – bring actions together into a smooth concerted way

4) Control – skill in the use of restraint, direction and coordination

5) Endurance – ability to tolerate stress or hardship

6) Strength – power to resist or exert force

7) Stamina – combination of endurance and strength

8) Speed – rate of motion

9) Power – might or influence

10) Reflex – end result of reception, transmission and reaction

11) Strategy – a careful plan or method to achieve a goal

Mentally, these character traits are nurtured & refined:

Respect

Discipline

Self Esteem

Confidence

Determination to Achieve Goals

氣

Qi (Energy)

Scholar Phase

Through practicing mental exercises (Qigong - vitality), one can better develop:

1) Relaxation of the muscles

2) Building of internal power

3) Strengthening of the organs

4) Improving the cardiopulmonary function

5) Strengthening the nerves

6) Improving vascular function

7) Can be practiced by the seriously ill

8) Help prevent injury to joints, ligaments & bones

9) Quicken recovery time from injuries & surgery

10) Building of athletic & martial arts power

11) Lessening of stress & balances emotions

12) Benefits sedentary individuals

Mentally, these concepts are comprehended & assimilated:
Human anatomy & physiology

Energy flow (Qi) with the energy meridians

Structural alignment of the skeletal & muscular systems

神

Shen (Spirit)

Sage Phase

Through practicing mediation exercises (Shen - consciousness), one can develop better understanding of:

1) The origin, nature, and character of things and beings

2) The human condition - study of human nature and conditions of life

3) The importance of communication on many different levels in order to share and disseminate wisdom

4) Sense of purpose

5) Making a difference

6) Self-less service to others

7) The inter-relationship between one another and how that can determine cause and effect

8) Our interaction between humans and the world (universe) we exist in

www.MindandBodyExercises.com

Weak People Create Hard Times

A new year comes, another new cycle begins. I think most would agree that this is true. Nature demonstrates patterns (universal truths) that have been around before humans and will be here after, such as seasons, weather patterns, natural disasters, etc. Humans being part of nature are subject to its patterns.

Hard times create strong men (people)

Strong men create good times

Good times create weak men

Weak men create hard times

Study and contemplate my graphic below, representing relationships between the universal truths of nature, whether manifested in the time of the day, time of the year, phases of the human lifecycle and consequently, how human nature (behavior) is often dictated by the natural environment that we all exist within.

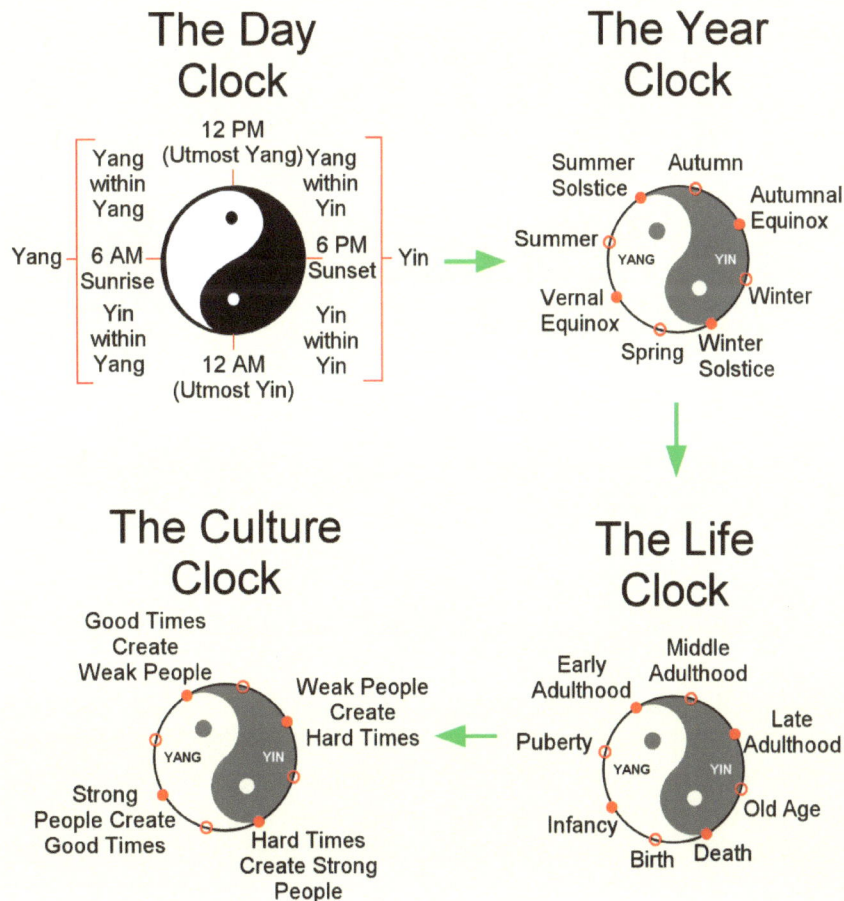

115

I feel we are all experiencing a watershed event, where we are just working through the above cycle. Some people may dispute this theory or cycle, but I think it holds true as compared similarly to the sun rising and setting, or the seasons of the year. So, I feel we are exactly where we are supposed to be whether viewed as a time for major political, societal and cultural changes, re-evaluation of our moral compasses, world health crises or the advancement of technologies - everything exists within cycles, and it all connects back to nature on some level.

You Can Only Give Out What You Yourself Have an Abundance Of

I have learned a bit about energetics over the years from my massage therapists as well as my martial arts/qigong teachers. During a massage, energy is depleted by the practitioner from the physical effort as well as the mental energy in trying to help and often heal the patient. This is very similar to emergency room doctors, nurses and others that can find themselves very run down or ill, while attempting to treat others. My understanding is that you can only give out what you yourself have an abundance of. If massage therapists and various other health-related professionals continue to draw from their well (life force, qi, prana) but fail to replenish it, they will soon have their own health issues. Exercise, diet and lifestyle choices all affect the practitioners' own well-being to replenish or retain their innate life force.

I learned early that you only have so much energy to give. You have to spend it correctly.

Eva Gabor

My understanding is that it really comes down to any occupation or activity that one individual loses some level of energy while trying to help another. It can be a parent taking care of a child, caretaker of a parent, teachers, etc. It is all about intent and energy expelled and received. This can lead to the topic of energy vampires and energy suns. We have probably all met people who, when walking into a room, drain the energy of all in their company. Or conversely, the person who comes in and brings up everyone's energy and puts a smile on everyone's' face. Yin and yang in all things!

Scarcity vs. Abundance
by Michael Hyatt

SCARCITY	ABUNDANCE
There is never enough	There is always more where that came from
Stingy with knowledge, contacts and compassion	Happy to share knowledge, contacts and compassion
Default to suspicion; hard to build rapport	Default to rapport and build trust easily
Resent competition. Makes the pie smaller, them weaker	Welcome competitors. Makes the pie larger, them stronger
Ask self: How can I get by with less than expected?	Ask self: How can I give more than expected?
Pessimistic about the future; tough times are ahead	Optimistic about the future; the best is yet to come
They think small, avoiding risk	They think big, embracing risk
They are entitled and fearful	They are thankful and confident

SOURCE: http://michaelhyatt.com/064-two-kinds-of-thinkers-podcast.html
Compiled by Chuck Frey, author of *Up Your Impact* - http://upyourimpact.com

Glossary

Abdominal breathing – effective, diaphragmatic breathing that fills your lungs fully, reaches all the way down to your abdomen, slows your breathing rate, and helps you relax.

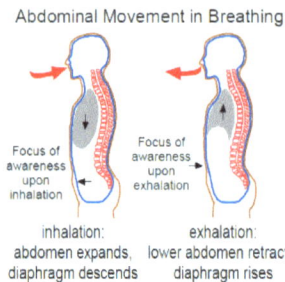

Abdominal Movement in Breathing

Focus of awareness upon inhalation

Focus of awareness upon exhalation

inhalation: abdomen expands, diaphragm descends

exhalation: lower abdomen retracts, diaphragm rises

Bagua (or Pa Kua) / 8-trigrams - eight symbols used in Daoist philosophy to represent the fundamental principles of reality, seen as a range of eight interrelated concepts. Each consists of three lines, each line either "broken" or "unbroken," respectively representing yin or yang.

Ch'ien Heaven
Tui Valley / Lake
Sun Wind
Li Fire
K'an Water
Chen Thunder
K'un Earth
Ken Mountain

The Brass Basin – sits within the lower abdomen, touching at the navel in the front, between L2 & L3 vertebrae in the back and the perineum at the base.

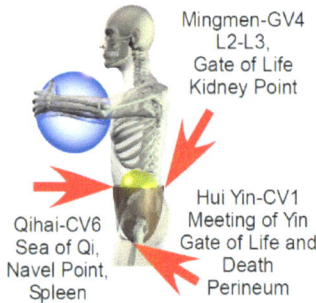

Mingmen-GV4 L2-L3, Gate of Life Kidney Point

Qihai-CV6 Sea of Qi, Navel Point, Spleen

Hui Yin-CV1 Meeting of Yin Gate of Life and Death Perineum

Bubbling Well - an energetic point located in the sole of the foot, slightly in front of the arch between the 2nd and 3rd toe. In the meridian system it is the same as the Kidney 1 point.

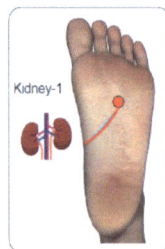

Kidney-1

Dan Tian - 3 energy centers Lower Dan Tian (1 of 3) - also known as the "sea of qi," is positioned below and behind the naval encompassing your lower bowl and is closely related to jing (or physical essence).

Shen-Spirit Upper Dantian (Field of Light)

Qi-Energy Middle Dantian (Field of Vibration)

Jing-Essence Lower Dantian (Field of Heat)

Daoyin, DaoYi, Daoist Yoga, Qigong – all names for energy exercises, with specific postures, little or no physical body movement and mindful regulated breathing patterns.

Feng Shui – translated into 'wind and water'; it is a Chinese philosophical system that teaches how to balance the energies in any given space.

FENG wind

SHUI water

Conception Vessel (Ren Mai) – flows up the midline of the front of the body and governs all of the yin channels. The Conception Vessel is connected to the Thrusting and Yin Linking vessels.

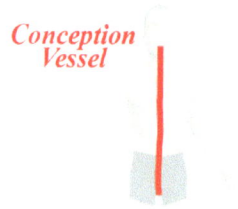

Conception Vessel

Governing Vessel (Du Mai) - flows up the midline of the back and governs all the Yang channels.

Governing Vessel

General Yu Fei – creator of the 8 Pieces of Brocade set.

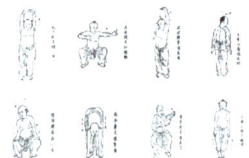

118

Controlling Cycle – the controlling or regulating sequence of the 5 element cycle. Wood controls Earth; Earth controls Water; Water controls Fire; Fire controls Metal; Metal controls Wood

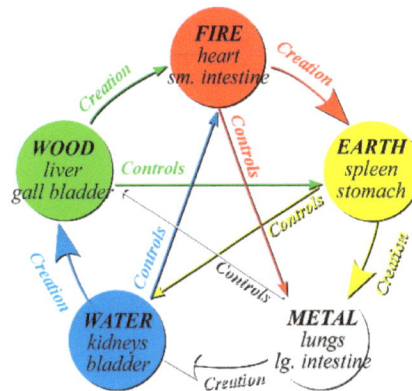

Generating Cycle – the creative sequence of the 5 element cycle. Wood generates Fire; Fire generates Earth; Earth generates Metal; Metal generates Water; Water generates Wood.

Horary Cycle - 24 Hour Qi Flow Though the Meridians; This cycle is known as the Horary cycle or the Circadian Clock. As Qi (energy) makes its way through the meridians, each meridian in turn with its associated organ, has a two-hour period during which it is at maximum energy.

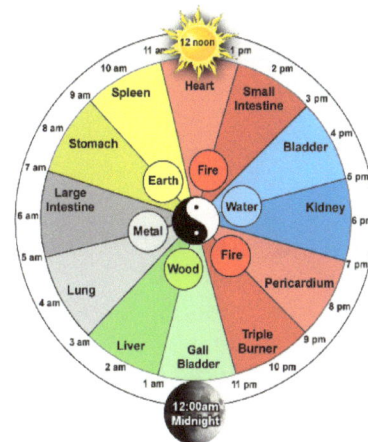

Jing Well - The Jing (Well) points are 1 of 5 of The Five Element Points (shu) of the 12 energy meridians. They are located on the fingers and toes of the four extremities. These points are thought to be where the Qi of the meridians emerges and begins moving towards the trunk of the body. These are of upmost importance in that these points can help restore balance within the energy flow throughout the human body.

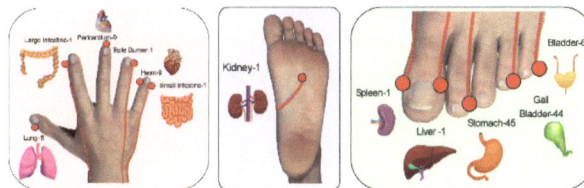

Meridians - a meridian is an 'energy highway' in the human body. There are 12 meridians and each is paired with an organ. Qi energy flows through these meridians or energy highways.

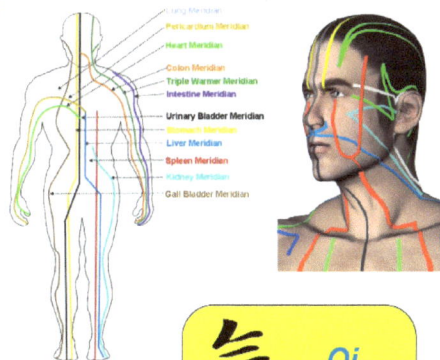

Qigong - or Chi Kung, is breathing exercises, with little or no body movement, that can adjust the brain waves to the Alpha state. When the mind is relaxed, the body chemistry changes and promotes natural healing.

San Jiao (Triple Burner/Heater) – is a meridian line that regulates respiration, digestion and elimination. It is responsible for the movement and transformation of various solids and fluids throughout the system, as well as for the production and circulation of nourishing and protective energy.

Upper Burner	**WEI QI**
Middle Burner	**YING QI**
Lower Burner	**YUAN QI**

119

Nine Gates - the energy gates in your body are major relay stations where the strength of your Qi are regulated. These gates are located at joints or, more precisely, in the actual space between the bones of a joint. The nine gates are located at the shoulder, elbow and wrists, hip, knee and ankles, and along the cervical, the thoracic, and the lumbar spine.

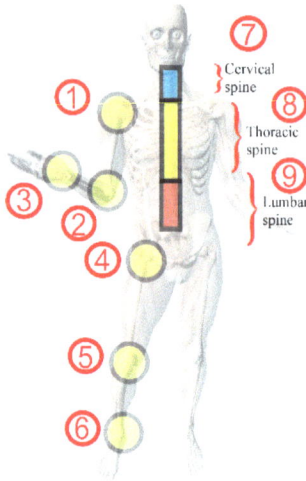

Seven Energy Centers – also known as chakras, are energy points in the subtle body that start at the base of the spinal column, continue through the sacral, solar plexus, heart, throat, eyebrow and end in the midst of the head vertex at the crown.

Three Treasures – Jing, Qi & Shen

Jing – (essence) the physical, yin and most dense of the Three Treasures. Think of Jing as a candle, specifically the quality and quantity of the wax.

Qi, chi or ki - (energy/breath) the energetic, vital force within all living things and it the most refined Treasure. Think of Qi as the burning flame of the candle.

Shen – (consciousness or spirit, is the most subtle of the Three Treasures and is the vitality behind Jing and Qi. Think of Shen as the light or illumination produced from the flame.

Six Healing Sounds – auditory sounds used for clearing internal (yin) organs and other tissues of stagnant Qi.

Metal - Hissss	Water - Chuuu	Wood - Shiiii	Fire - Haaaa	Earth - Hoooo	6th Qi - Heeee
Lungs Lg. Intestine	Kidneys Bladder	Liver Gall Bladder	Heart Sm. Intestine	Spleen Stomach	Pericardium Triple Burner

The 3 Hearts – Heart, abdomen, calves: The first heart is the heart in your chest for the oxygenation of the blood. Lower abdominal breathing is considered the second heart for circulation of fluid, Qi and digestion. The third heart is the calf muscles for re-circulation of the blood.

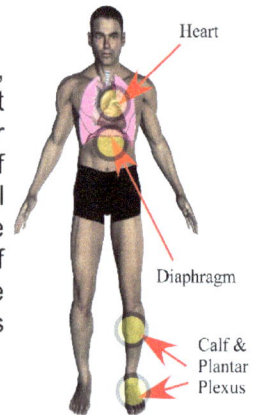

Heart
Diaphragm
Calf & Plantar Plexus

Small Circuit – the linking two energy pathways that run along the midline of the body into a cycling loop. The "fire pathway", Du Mai (Governing Vessel), extends up the back and the other, Ren Mai (Conception Vessel), down the front of the body.

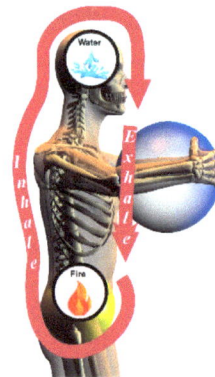

Water
Exhale
Inhale
Fire

Vessels – there are 8 extraordinary vessels that function as reservoirs of Qi for the Twelve Regular Meridians.

Conception	
Thrusting	**4 Yin Vessels**
Yin Linking	
Yin Heel	
Governing	
Belt	**4 Yang Vessels**
Yang Linking	
Yang Heel	

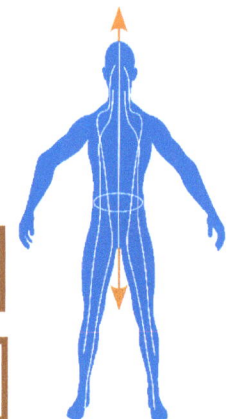

Taoism - (sometimes Daoism) is a philosophical or ethical tradition of Chinese origin, or faith of Chinese exemplification, that emphasizes living in harmony with the Tao (or Dao). The term Tao means "way", "path", or the "principle".

120

The Void (Supreme Mystery)

Wuji – ultimate stillness, the beginning of creation.

Yang Qi - yang refers to aspects or manifestations of Qi that are relatively positive: Also-immaterial, amorphous, expanding, hollow, light, ascending, hot, dry, warming, bright, aggressive, masculine and active.

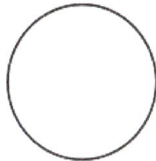

Yin Qi - yin refers to aspects or manifestations of Qi that are relatively negative: Also - material, substantial, condensing, solid, heavy, descending, cold, moist, cooling, dark, female, passive and quiescent.

Taijitu -The term taijitu in modern Chinese is commonly used to mean the simple "divided circle" form (), but it may refer to any of several schematic diagrams that contain at least one circle with an inner pattern of symmetry representing yin and yang.

Yi – intellect, manifests as spirit-infused intelligence and understanding.

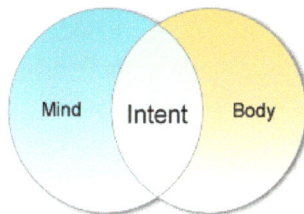

Baihui point - Governing Vessel 20 (GV 20). Sits on the crown of the head.

Jade Pillow – located at the top of the cervical vertebrae (C1).

Great Hammer – located on the midline at the base of the neck, between seventh cervical vertebra and first thoracic vertebra.

Mingmen point – Conception Vessel 6 (CV6), the 'Sea of Qi' located on the lower abdomen.

Qihai point – Conception Vessel 6 (CV6), the 'Sea of Qi' located on the lower abdomen.

Hui Yin point – Conception Vessel 1 (CV1), also known as the base chakra, is located between the genitals and the anus; the part of the body called the perineum.

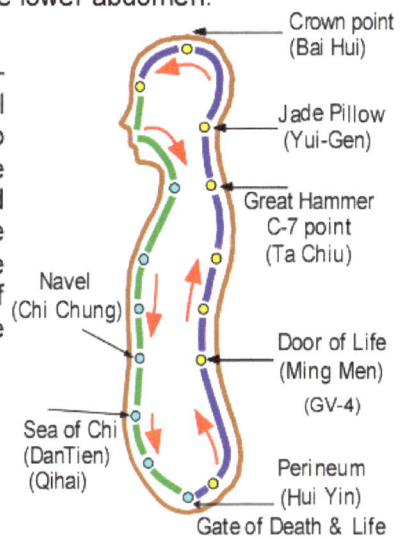

Wu Xing or 5 Elements -
The 5 Element theory is a major component of thought within Traditional Chinese Medicine (TCM). Each element represents natural aspects within our world. Natural cycles and interrelationships between these elements, is the basis for this theory. These elements have corresponding relationships within our environment as well as within our own being.

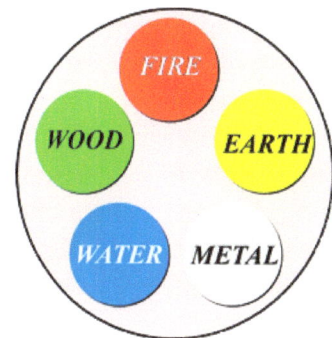

Zang-Fu organs – solid, yin organs are Zang – yang and hollow organs are Fu.

About the Instructor, Author & Artist - Jim Moltzan

My fitness training started at the age of 16 and has continued for almost 45 years. During that time, I attended high school, then college, and worked 2 jobs all while pursuing further training in martial arts and other fitness methods. Many years ago, I started up an additional business to help finance my next goal of owning my own school. I moved to Florida from the Midwest to make this goal a reality. Having owned two wellness and martial arts schools, I have surpassed what I once believed to be my potential. At this stage in my life, I have chosen not to open any more schools, as I found the business aspects took too much focus away from my true passion: training and teaching others.

Beyond my professional endeavors, I am also a husband and father of two grown children. I believe that we must be prepared to work hard mentally, physically and financially to earn our good health and well-being. Not only for ourselves but for our families as well. Good health always comes at a cost whether in time, effort, cost, sacrifice or some combination of the previous.

I returned to college in my later 50's, to pursue my BS in Holistic Health (wellness and alternative medicine). My degree program covered many wide-ranging topics such as anatomy and physiology, meditation, massage, nutrition, herbology, chemistry, biology, history and basis of various medical modalities such as allopathic, Traditional Chinese Medicine, Ayurveda/yoga, naturopathy, chiropractic, and complimentary alternative methods. I also studied religion, mythology of the world, stress relief/management as well as sociology, psychology (human behavior) and cultural issues associated with better health and wellness.

Most of the movements I teach and write about originate from Chinese martial arts. The Qigong (breathing work) is from Chinese Kung Fu and the Korean Dong Han medical Qigong lineage. I have also gained much knowledge of Traditional Chinese Medicine (TCM) from many TCM practitioners, martial arts masters, teachers and peers. This includes many techniques and practices of acupressure (reflexology, auricular, Jing Well, etc.), acupuncture, moxibustion as well as preparation of some herbal remedies and extracts for conditioning and injuries. I have been studying for over 20 years with Zen Wellness, learning medical Qigong as well as other Eastern methods of fitness, philosophy and self-cultivation. I have been recognized as a "Gold Coin" master instructor having trained and taught others for at least

10000 hours or roughly over 35 years. The core fitness movements are from Kung Fu and its forms in Tai Chi, Baguazhang, Dao Yin and Ship Pal Gi (Korean Kung Fu and weapons training). Each martial art has mental, physical and spiritual aspects that can complement and enhance one another. The more ways that you can move your body and engage your mind, the better it is for your overall health.

Physical health, mental well-being and the relationships within our lives; are these the most cherished aspects of our existence? Yet, how much effort do we put towards improving these areas on a daily basis?

Many have used martial arts and other mind-body methods of training as methods of learning to see one's character as others see them. I feel that I can offer the priceless qualities of truth, honor and integrity with my instruction. You must seek the right teacher for you, because in time a student can become similar to their teacher. Through the training that I have experienced and offer to others, an individual can understand and hopefully reach their full potential.

By developing self-discipline to continuously execute and perfect sets of movements, an individual can start to understand not only how they work physically but also mentally and emotionally. You can find your strengths and your weaknesses and improve them both. Through disciplined training, one not only enhances physical abilities but also cultivates mental resilience, allowing them to achieve their fullest potential in all areas of life.

I have co-authored a book, produced numerous other books and journals, graphic charts and study guides related to the mind and body connection and how it relates to martial arts, fitness, and self-improvement. A few hundred of my classes and lectures are viewable on YouTube.com.

Lineage

- o Recognized as a 1000 and 10,000-hour student and teacher

- o Earned gold coins through the Doh Yi Masters and Zen Wellness program

- o Earned a 5th degree in Korean Kung Fu through the Dong Han lineage

Education

Bachelor of Science in Holistic Medicine - Vermont State University

Books Available Through Amazon

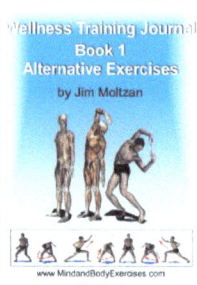

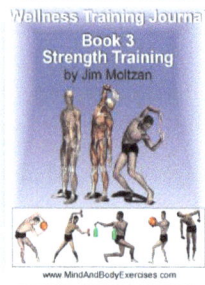

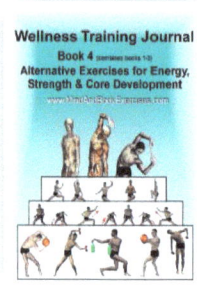

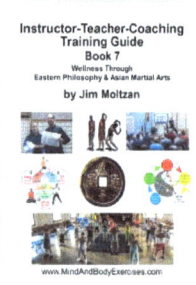

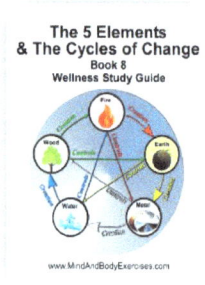

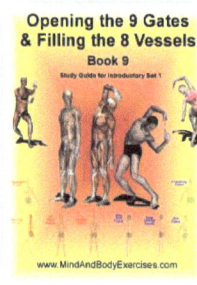

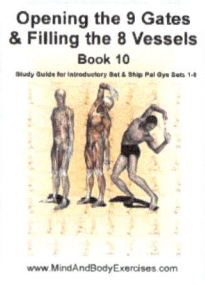

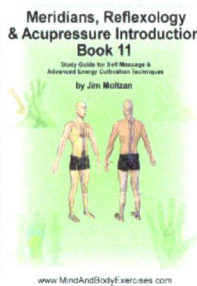

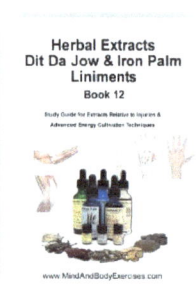

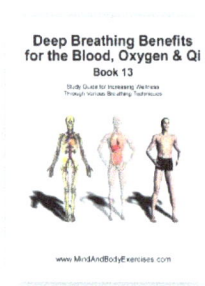

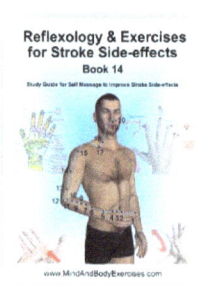

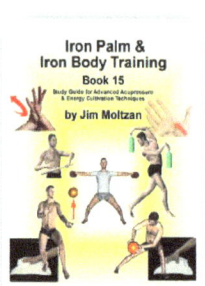

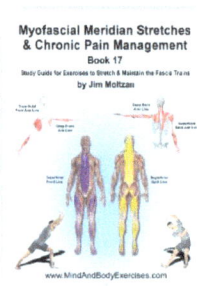

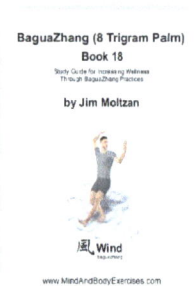

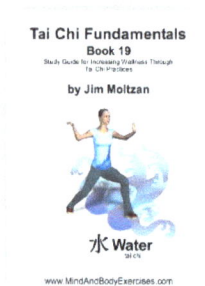

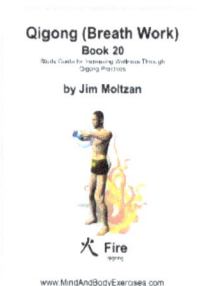

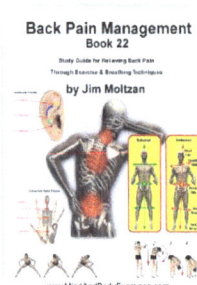

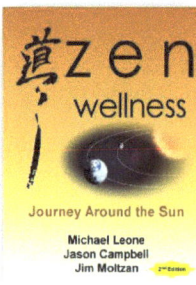

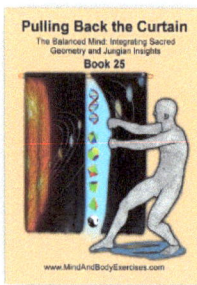

Wellness Training Journal
Book 1
Alternative Exercises
by Jim Moltzan

Wellness Training Journal
Book 2
Core Training
by Jim Moltzan
www.MindAndBodyExercises.com

Wellness Training Journal
Book 3
Strength Training
by Jim Moltzan
www.MindAndBodyExercises.com

Wellness Training Journal
Book 4 (exercises sets 1-3)
Alternative Exercises for Energy,
Strength & Core Development
www.MindAndBodyExercises.com

Wellness Journal
Book 5
Energizing Your Inner Strength
www.MindAndBodyExercises.com
Qi (energy) Gong (work) (cultivation)

Methods to Achieve
Better Wellness
Book 6
Wellness Study Guide
by Jim Moltzan
Jing · Qi · Shen

Instructor-Teacher-Coaching
Training Guide
Book 7
Wellness Through
Eastern Philosophy & Asian Martial Arts
by Jim Moltzan

The 5 Elements
& The Cycles of Change
Book 8
Wellness Study Guide
www.MindAndBodyExercises.com

Opening the 9 Gates
& Filling the 8 Vessels
Book 9
Study Guide for Introductory Set 1
www.MindAndBodyExercises.com

Opening the 9 Gates
& Filling the 8 Vessels
Book 10
Study Guide for Introductory Set & Ship Pal Gye Sets 1-8

Meridians, Reflexology
& Acupressure Introduction
Book 11
Study Guide for Self Massage &
Advanced Energy Cultivation Techniques
by Jim Moltzan
www.MindAndBodyExercises.com

Herbal Extracts
Dit Da Jow & Iron Palm
Liniments
Book 12
Study Guide for Extracts Relative to Injuries &
Advanced Energy Cultivation Techniques
www.MindAndBodyExercises.com

Deep Breathing Benefits
for the Blood, Oxygen & Qi
Book 13
Study Guide for Increasing Wellness
Through Various Breathing Techniques
www.MindAndBodyExercises.com

Reflexology & Exercises
for Stroke Side-effects
Book 14
Study Guide for Self Massage to Improve Stroke Side-effects
www.MindAndBodyExercises.com

Iron Palm &
Iron Body Training
Book 15
Study Guide for Advanced Acupressure
& Energy Cultivation Techniques
by Jim Moltzan
www.MindAndBodyExercises.com

Myofascial Meridian Stretches
& Chronic Pain Management
Book 17
Study Guide for Exercises to Stretch & Maintain the Fascia Trains
by Jim Moltzan
www.MindAndBodyExercises.com

BaguaZhang (8 Trigram Palm)
Book 18
Study Guide for Increasing Wellness
Through BaguaZhang Practices
by Jim Moltzan
Wind
www.MindAndBodyExercises.com

Tai Chi Fundamentals
Book 19
Study Guide for Increasing Wellness Through
Tai Chi Practices
by Jim Moltzan
Water
www.MindAndBodyExercises.com

Qigong (Breath Work)
Book 20
Study Guide for Increasing Wellness Through
Qigong Practices
by Jim Moltzan
Fire
www.MindAndBodyExercises.com

Wind & Water Makes Fire
Book 21
Study Guide for Increasing Wellness Through
BaguaZhang, Tai Chi & Qigong Practices
by Jim Moltzan
Wind Fire Water
www.MindAndBodyExercises.com

Back Pain Management
Book 22
Study Guide for Relieving Back Pain
Through Exercise & Breathing Techniques
by Jim Moltzan
www.MindAndBodyExercises.com

zen wellness
Journey Around the Sun
Michael Leone
Jason Campbell
Jim Moltzan
2nd Edition

Internal Alchemy
study guide for mind, body
and spiritual cultivation
Zen Wellness special edition

Pulling Back the Curtain
The Balanced Mind: Integrating Sacred
Geometry and Jungian Insights
Book 25
www.MindAndBodyExercises.com

Whole Health
Wisdom:
Navigating
Holistic Wellness

Books Titles by Jim Moltzan

On Amazon

Book 1 - Alternative Exercises

Book 2 - Core Training

Book 3 - Strength Training

Book 4 - Combo of 1-3

Book 5 - Energizing Your Inner Strength

Book 6 - Methods to Achieve Better Wellness

Book 7 - Coaching & Instructor Training Guide

Book 8 - The 5 Elements & the Cycles of Change

Book 9 - Opening the 9 Gates & Filling 8 Vessels - Intro Set 1

Book 10 - Opening the 9 Gates & Filling 8 Vessels-sets 1 to 8

Book 11 - Meridians, Reflexology & Acupressure

Book 12 - Herbal Extracts, Dit Da Jow & Iron Palm Liniments

Book 13 - Deep Breathing Benefits for the Blood, Oxygen & Qi

Book 14 - Reflexology for Stroke Side Effects:

Book 15 - Iron Body & Iron Palm

Book 17 - Fascial Train Stretches & Chronic Pain Management

Book 18 - BaguaZhang

Book 19 - Tai Chi Fundamentals

Book 20 - Qigong (breath-work)

Book 21 - Wind & Water Make Fire

Book 22 - Back Pain Management

Book 23 - Journey Around the Sun-2nd Edition

Book 24 - Graphic Reference Book - Internal Alchemy

Book 25 – Pulling Back the Curtain

Book 26 - Whole Health Wisdom: Navigating Holistic Wellness

Other Products

Laminated Charts 8.5" x 11" or 11" x 17" - over 200 various graphics (check the website)

Qigong - Chi Kung
SKU: ChiKung

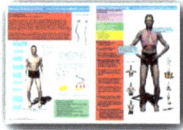

The human body is made up of bones, muscles, and organs amongst other components. Veins, arteries and capillaries carry blood and nutrients throughout to all of the systems and components. Additionally, 12 major energy medians carry the body's energy, "life force" also known as "chi". Ones chi is stored in the lower Dan Tien. Daily emotional imbalances accumulate tension and stress gradually affecting all of the body's systems. Each discomfort, nuisance, irritation or grudge continues to tighten and squeeze the flow of the life force. This is where "dis-ease" claims its foothold.

Strengthen Your Back (set #1)
SKU: StrengthenYourBack1

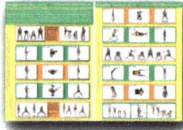

Good health of the lower back starts with good posture. The following set of exercises develop strength and flexibility which improve posture. Strength in the back, hips and abdominals provide a strong cage that houses the internal organs. Flexibility in these areas helps to maintain good blood circulation to the organs and lower body. Lengthening of the spine while exercising reduces stress and tension on the nervous system.

Broadsword 1-10
SKU: Broadsword

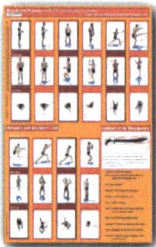

Broadsword training develops the body, mind and spirit well beyond that which can gained from empty hand training alone. The Broadsword has many different sets to be mastered utilizing quick, fluid and precise movements.

Ship Pal Gye set 7 (Kung Fu stance training)
SKU: ShipPalGye7

SHIP PAL GYE or Ship Par Gay, is a Korean version of Chinese Shaolin Lohan Qigong, meaning "18 chi movements" or what were supposedly the original 18 drills that Bodhidharma introduced to the Shaolin monks. It is reputed to be the basis for the Shaolin Kung Fu, which in turn, greatly influenced the developments of all branches of Asian fighting arts.

Noble Stances
SKU: NobleStances

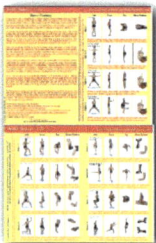

Noble stances are a combination of various stances from different styles of Chinese martial arts. Stances, in this case, meaning correct placement of the feet, knees, hips, and arm positions relative to ones center of gravity. Executing static positions and holding the particular body positions for anyway from a few seconds to several minutes reaps many benefits foremost being able to cultivate a strong and healthy core.

126

Contacts

For more information regarding charts, products, classes and instruction:

www.MindAndBodyExercises.com
info@MindAndBodyExercises.com

www.youtube.com/c/MindandBodyExercises
www.MindAndBodyExercises.wordpress.com

407-234-0119

Social Media:

Facebook: MindAndBodyExercises
Instagram: MindAndBodyExercises
Twitter: MindAndBodyExercise

Jim Moltzan - Mind and Body Exercises
522 Hunt Club Blvd. #305
Apopka, FL 32703

Website

Blog

YouTube Channel

www.ingramcontent.com/pod-product-compliance
Lightning Source LLC
Chambersburg PA
CBHW060858270326
41935CB00003B/18